Rebirth in Washington

Rebirth in Washington

The Christian Impact in the Nation's Capital

By Wallace Henley

GOOD NEWS PUBLISHERS
Westchester, Illinois 60153

TABLE OF CONTENTS

PART I:
THE NEED

PART II:
MISSIONARIES TO THE MIGHTY

INTRODUCTION

It was a mistake to pick up the galley proofs. Good News Publishers had asked me to write an introduction to Wallace Henley's book and had sent the manuscript. The morning it arrived my desk was covered with work which I had planned to get to immediately, but the writing of Wallace Henley attracted me. I know him well enough to appreciate his ability to communicate. That he wrote about the city I love, Washington, D.C., intrigued me.

I decided, therefore, just to glance at the manuscript and then set it aside for a more convenient time. That was a mistake. It had never happened to me before, but this book drew me into itself so irresistibly that I literally did not put it down until I had read it through to the end. Nor did I regret having done so.

Mr. Henley's autobiographical style presents, in living color, an authentic and vivid picture of Christian influence in the capital city. Though the book is intensely personal, the author sustains careful objectivity in describing diverse Christian works covering a broad spectrum of shapes and strategies. (He was, however, far too generous in his description of this writer's ministry.)

The book opens with a remarkably frank and graphic view of the milieu that is metropolitan Washington. From the perspective of an insider, he presents an unusually candid exposure of things as they are. It smacks almost of investigative reporting. The author certainly could not be accused of cover up.

He sees the deepest issue in Washington as "not political nor economic nor military crisis, but spiritual crisis." This conviction is adequately supported with quotations from some of the most perceptive public personalities. "The crisis of the time," said Senator Moynihan, "is not political; it is in essence religious. It is a crisis of large numbers of intensely moral, even godly, people who no longer hope for God...."

He presents thoughtfully, from a biblical point of view, the built-in weaknesses and dangers of non-representative political systems. I found this section to be very stimulating. He avoids, however, sanctifying any system, arguing for the sovereignty of the people while, at the same time, warning of the perils of civil religion. His analysis of the limitations and accountability of all human government is especially relevant. He demands that those in authority model the morality they are appointed by God to protect.

> When a ruling power no longer acknowledges that its ruling responsibilities come from God and belong to Him, then that authority has removed itself from God and has thus cut itself off from its own base of authority. It is no more capable of

exercising its purpose than a flashlight without
batteries!

The author's bold, honest, penetrating review of
the Washington establishment does not lead to despair. He demonstrates the need for a spiritual re-
crudescence and in the last half of the book takes a
comprehensive look at varied ministries which are
exerting a growing impact on the nation's power
center and its powerful elite.

Here is a compelling exposition—biblically,
theologically, morally, politically and practically—
of the nation's dilemma, the relevance of the Gospel
of Jesus Christ to it and some of the means God is
using to resolve it.

Richard C. Halverson

PREFACE

"The joy of writing is in having written." So says a friend of mine, a college English professor. But I must confess that the joy of writing this book was not limited to holding the finished manuscript in my hand, feeling its weight, knowing it was done. The joy ran all through the writing process.

One reason is that I love Washington—an affair of affection that was dimmed only briefly during the Watergate tribulation. But the love has long since returned, and I enjoy walking back through the city mentally and physically and talking about its people.

But there is a much more basic reason for my delight in writing of ministry in Washington: I am a product of such ministry. I was not touched by every effort at outreach detailed in this book. But many of the Christians who so profoundly affected my life in their witness are involved in even those ministries in which I was not directly caught up. So I think I understand something of their spirit.

In the years since I left Washington, I have given a good deal of study to the biblical teachings on government, authority, power, freedom and human institutions. I wish I had done that before serving on the White House staff! For I have been over-whelmed at times with the relevance of Scripture on these issues as they are manifested in the twentieth century. From Nimrod and his city in Genesis, to the soundings of the prophets, to the compassion of Jesus for centurions, to the theological dissertations of Paul, the Bible speaks directly again and again on the systems whereby human beings order their societies. It is the failure to understand what Planet Earth's Operations Manual says about government that causes such confusion and heartache.

That explains the structure of this book. In Part I, I have sought to touch this biblical teaching, and show why it is so important that people do give themselves to Christian ministry in Washington. There are, after all, Christians who yet have the isolationist attitude of the early church Father, Tertulian, who held that God's people ought to be totally removed from affairs of state.

Then, in Part II, I have tried to show a little of what is going on in Christian ministry in Washington. Let me stress the word "little." Even if someone attempted a complete anthology of Washington ministries by Christians, that author would fail. For there are so many things going on—so many quiet things—that it may be some of the greatest works are being overlooked in books like this.

But I write with the hope that Christians everywhere will pray for and support financially Christian projects in the United States capital.

I have not tried to suggest here that all the programs written about are doing all they should do, nor doing what they do perfectly. Some disagree with what others are doing. There is a smattering of competitive feeling. But as an observer—now from

Preface

outside Washington—and as a person who has been touched by the work of Christians there, I am grateful for the diversity of approach and attitude!

Wallace Henley
January, 1977

PART I
The Need

CHAPTER I

'Come over to the White House'

Someone had turned over a basket of gold nuggets, and now they glimmered in the soft light of the setting sun. At least that was the way the ivory buildings of Washington looked from the window of a Boeing 727 settling into her landing pattern.

Ground control had vectored us to my favorite approach into Washington National. We had swung out toward the west in the approach, over the Virginia and then the Maryland suburbs. Below I had seen the Washington Beltway snaking around the western perimeter. Fairfax, Alexandria, Falls Church had all passed below. Then we had skimmed over lavish homes bordering the Potomac. Picking up the river, we traced its route toward Washington National.

Through the windows on the left side of the airplane cabin, the ponderous buildings and monuments of Washington had come into view. The Kennedy Center appeared as a crate left by a barge at a Georgetown Port. To its rear loomed the contemporary barrels of the Watergate complex. A few seconds and the White House and Old Executive Office Building edged into view. Then the Washington Monument, the Mall and the array of mausoleum-looking buildings crowned by the Capitol.

I had not been in Washington long. The city was still unknown to me. I wondered about the unseen people scurrying about in those buildings. They were filing and typing and deciding and flirting. I knew that if their jobs were like mine, they were looking at clocks and calendars, almost suffocating under deadlines and pressures.

My mind focused on those people my eyes could not pick out: What were their lives really like? What did they do and think when they were not plodding through their days like pre-programmed humanoids? Did their minds ever run beyond filing cabinets and reports-in-triplicate to, say, spiritual things? Was there anyone in Washington who cared about these people? Now it was occurring to me that I was one of them. Was there anyone in Washington who cared spiritually about *me?*

Now I got a new impression about the buildings sliding under the wing of the aircraft. The mausoleum analogy, I decided, might not be far from wrong. Maybe they were like the whited sepulchres Jesus talked about: outwardly gleaming, but inwardly filled with dead men's bones.

It would be nearly a year later before those questions began to be answered for me. And in the intervening year, I would become one of those drowned in the sea of the mundane, choked off from spiritual interests and concerns in a period in my life when they would be critical.

Back home in Birmingham, there had been the normal, "local kid strikes it big" stories when I had gone to work in a White House-related job. I knew that I was essentially only a bureaucrat—slightly glorified, perhaps, because of the White House connection. But the fact was I spent most of my time in a windowless cubbyhole in those first months, analyzing reports and writing more of them.

On this particular afternoon, I was returning from the South, where I had met with groups of citizens concerned about public education. As soon as I returned to my office, I would pull together their thoughts and ideas into still another report which I had no assurance anyone would take seriously enough to respond to with action.

Yet such materials always had to be in by yesterday. It was now Friday, and I knew the weekend would be spent working away, completing a report that just might move a feather. The upshot of it would be that I would be cut off from the church another weekend. I had not yet noticed it, but my spiritual life was getting buried under a ton of paper.

The airplane had now lined up with the runway and was sinking toward the ground. I thought about the churches and Christian groups that I had followed over the years. They were active in ministries to jails, downtown rescue missions and their derelicts, to drug addicts, to the economically deprived, to juvenile delinquents—in general to the down-and-outer. Was anyone burdened for the bureaucrat? Was there anyone aiming a ministry at the up-and-outer whose pride was as hard to penetrate as the cynical bitterness of the down-and-outer?

The jetliner bounded slightly as its wheels socked the runway. I was soon to learn much more about the city in which I had just landed. I would understand more deeply than I thought possible the unique spiritual needs of leaders and government workers. And I would discover a compassionate set of ministries being carried out by Christians seeking to minister to such folk.

One of the things I would learn was that Washington was a mission field the size of a small state, in population at least. According to one conjecture, if all the federal employees in Washington were lined up across the country, beginning at the base of the Washington Monument, the line would stretch to the Golden Gate Bridge!

These people battle the Shirley Highway and Independence Avenue and Memorial Bridge and the transit company to get to their awesome-looking buildings. Once inside they are muffled from the street preacher's voice, cut off from the tract-passer. After long days and 90-minute wars with the traffic, some of them fan out to the 500 cocktail parties thrown in Washington each day.

Who's burdened for the bureaucrat?

The answer, as we shall see, is that there are some innovative Christians burdened for government officials and workers. And they are trying to do something about that burden!

Momentarily, we will look at Romans 13, where Paul says the government official is the minister of God. Yet everything in the world of the bureaucrat seems to tug his gaze earthward rather than heavenward. Keeping one's sanity sometimes becomes a major operation in itself.

Take, for example, the aide to a certain senator. I heard about him and trembled while I was in the ranks of the bureaucrat. His boss, the senator, had conversed with a supporter about a certain issue. Since the senator was on a swing home and the aide was left in Washington, the aide did not hear the conversation firsthand. Nevertheless, in the ways of bureaucracies everywhere, the aide would wind up the main conversant in a conversation that took place several hundred miles out of his hearing!

After the senator had returned to Washington, the supporter wrote him a letter, disagreeing with the senator's position on the issue. The senator called in his aide, told him how to reply, and the aide drafted a letter for the senator's signature. The supporter, however, had a few counterpoints to make, and did so. Again the senator called in the aide, and the aide wrote yet another letter for the senator's signature. This time the supporter called in and talked to the aide. "Just put my thoughts down in a memo for the senator to read," instructed the supporter. The aide did that. Immediately the aide was told by the senator to draft a reply "along the lines we've discussed before." By the time this process was completed, the aide realized that he had been corresponding with himself, and that the supporter and senator had long ago dropped out of the conversation they had instructed the beleaguered aide to conduct!

I was now strolling through another maze—the North Terminal of Washington National Airport. As I moved through the double automated doors, my eyes scanned for the black limousine from the White House which had been sent to pick me up. I would be able to pick it out of the herd of sleek black cars because of the special numerical designation on its license plate.

Soon I was in the car, its military driver skirting the streets with due precision. Far on the horizon, I could see the tower of the Washington Cathedral boldly asserting dominance over a portion of the city. I wondered. Was the dominance a trick of my eye, or was it symbolic of an impact being made by churches on the business of this hectic capital?

The car deposited me in the White House complex at a point referred to as "the ramp." One elevator ride up and a walk of half a city block, and I was at my desk in the Old Executive Office Building next door to the White House. I would not sit at that desk many more weeks until I would be drawn into the exciting ministry of Christians in Washington, a ministry which would someday be able to count me as one of those it affected most dramatically. But as I sat at the desk that day, I could not see that; I could only feel an overwhelming inadequacy and a near-devastating spiritual emptiness. It hurt, and on that day, the formless prayer the Holy Spirit was picking up in my subconscious, and transmitting to God's Throne, groaned out like this: "God, send somebody to help me." Maybe it was the Macedonian call, twentieth-century style, and could have been worded, "Come over to the White House and help us!"

Whatever the case, help was on its way, and that spiritual ministry could not have been aimed at a more appropriate place.

CHAPTER II

The Reverend Mr. Bureaucrat

On our last week in Washington, it occurred to us that we had never visited the Jefferson Memorial, which I had seen so often on those approaches into Washington National and on lumbering automobile passages over the Potomac. So on a bitterly cold Sunday afternoon in February, our family called on Mr. Jefferson.

We walked into the colonnaded rotunda surrounding the Goliath-size statue, and were nearly knocked down by the swift wind zipping through the columns. I stood at the base of the statue, shivering. At the edge of my eye, I could see the White House, while Jefferson occupied center vision.

The Watergate at that point was only a series of rumors and tales appearing daily in the Washington press. But I had begun to sense that something was terribly wrong. The impression was forming—though I could not say why—that I was leaving Washington just before a cataclysmic political earthquake. All of this was passing through my mind as I craned my head upward to the bronzed face of Thomas Jefferson. And I began to weep. The feeling that had unleashed the tears was the impression that Thomas Jefferson's stone-frozen eyes on that chilling day seemed to see crisis. Not political nor economic nor military crisis, but spiritual crisis.

It was becoming increasingly clear that the pivotal issue of government in our time was spiritual in nature, namely this: *Can we survive as an orderly, democratic system if we do not grasp the fact and all its implications that the base of government and the validity of authority is God?* Tyrannies and anarchies are the fruit of wrong answers to that question. A government official who does not understand that he is the minister of God and that the official's authority is voided if cut off from its base cannot serve with a full appreciation of all it means for him to hold his job.

Daniel Patrick Moynihan, in a speech, seemed to catch the nature of this crisis. "The crisis of the time," said Senator Moynihan, "is not political; it is in essence religious. It is a crisis of large numbers of intensely moral, even godly, people who no longer hope for God. Hence, the quest for divinity assumes a secular form."

The implication in light of the Bible is that when a governing authority cuts itself off from the source of its authority in God, it tries to become its own authority base. And that is as great a contradiction as an electric plug trying to carry electricity when it has been jerked from the socket!

John Anderson described the political crisis like this: "How can one appeal to the Christian ethic as a morally unifying and aspiring force in a society which is at the same time repudiating the Christian religion?"

And Francis Schaeffer, in his sweeping work, *How Should We Then Live?*, reminds us that some of the most cherished fundamentals in the American Constitution grew out of the sturdy roots laid in Reformation thinking. Samuel Rutherford, a Scot, made a political application of biblical truth when, in 1644, he wrote a book entitled *Lex Rex*. Law was king, but only because the Bible was there with its absolutes as foundational. The message in Rutherford's time (1600-1661) was that even royalty came under the sovereignty of law.

Rutherford's thinking flowed into the Constitution through John Witherspoon, a Presbyterian clergyman who signed the Declaration of Independence. John Locke, a British philosopher, also influenced the principles expressed in the Constitution. But Locke, too, had been influenced by Rutherford's applications of biblical teaching to government.

Long before Rutherford, Witherspoon or Locke, the Apostle Paul had spoken the mind of God on government, authority and the official. In Romans 13, the Apostle wrote this:

> Let every soul be subject unto the higher powers. For there is no power but of God: the powers that be are ordained of God. Whosoever therefore resisteth the power, resisteth the ordinance of God:

and they that resist shall receive to themselves damnation. For rulers are not a terror to good works, but to the evil.... *For he is the minister of God to thee for good.* But if thou do that which is evil, be afraid: for he beareth not the sword in vain: *for he is the minister of God,* a revenger to execute wrath upon him that doeth evil.... For this cause pay ye tribute also: *for they are God's ministers* [italics added].

Three times in that passage Paul refers to the government official as the minister of God. His authority comes from God, as well as the definitions by which he knows what constitutes legitimate power. Hence, he is also responsible before God.

The governing official is to see that his right to authority is a gift from God. As we shall see momentarily when we look at Ephesians 6, authority is given by God as the essential weapon against Satan's basic work of disorganization, the creation of chaos. The ultimate reason God grants the gift of authority is to restrain the demons of chaos, and the spirit of antichrist, which is lawlessness and disorder (II Thessalonians 2:7).

The great error of the "divine right" potentates of the age of royalty was in their prostitution of the idea of authority as a gift from God. They prostituted it when they inferred that such a gift was limited to certain families. Worse still, though they readily saw all the privileges of the gift of authority they failed to understand that when God gives immense privilege and giftedness, He also gives great responsibility. When they were cut off from this legitimate power source, they were no longer authoritative.

The Reverend Mr. Bureaucrat

If the gift of authority is ultimately for the restraint of demonic chaos, there are some specific tasks for those in authority, continues Paul. Wherever there is the acceptance of God's gift, there must be acceptance of the corresponding responsibility of stewardship which accompanies the gift.

Among other things, the government official is responsible for encouraging good conduct. Paul spells it out: "For rulers are not a terror to good works, but to the evil. Wilt thou not then be afraid of the power? do that which is good, and thou shalt have praise of the same: For he is the minister of God to thee for good" (Romans 13:3-4).

The bitter experience of Richard Nixon may be a graphic illustration of how this principle applies. Nixon lost his power when it became clear that lies had come from the Oval Office itself. The ability of the office to encourage good conduct in people had been stifled by its own bad conduct, and that was the point at which the pressure on Nixon to resign became most intense.

Paul notes another very specific ministry of the governing authority: he is to punish the wrongdoer. Romans 13:4 continues like this: "But if thou do that which is evil, be afraid; for he beareth not the sword in vain; for he is the minister of God, a revenger to execute wrath upon him that doeth evil."

This, of course, demands that the governing authority be just itself and work for justice in the society over which it has stewardship. Here particularly, the work of restraining chaos is carried out. But as we shall see later, a governing authority is able to execute justice properly only when that authority understands itself to be under the sovereignty of God.

In summary, then, we conclude that the governing official must understand that his authority is a gift from God, given for the purpose of restraining the work of the "lawless one" in society, and that the official is to encourage good conduct and see to it that justice is brought against the outlaw.

But what happens when a government fails to understand that its authority is under God?

Just this: When a governing power ceases to operate under authority which is based on the sovereignty of God, *that power becomes invalid.* How can an authority restrain the work of the "lawless one" when the authority itself is lawless? This is the base of revolution. But even a revolution is invalid which does not understand that it must submit itself to the authority of God. World affairs in the age of "liberation" movements would be quite different if revolutionaries would understand this crucial point. The world would be spared the heartache of terrorism and anarchy if the leaders of revolution could grasp the fact that, no matter how just the cause, their *work* is not just unless they have submitted themselves to God's rulership. A revolutionary with no authority above himself becomes a tyrant!

When a ruling power no longer acknowledges that its ruling responsibilities come from God and belong to Him, then that authority has removed itself from God and has thus cut itself off from its own base of authority. It is no more capable of exercising its purpose than a flashlight without batteries!

In essence, the governing power cut off from God has ceased to be an instrument of God, which is its very reason for being. It becomes idolatrous, attempting to be its own moral and legal base.

In Acts 5, we see the reaction of the apostles in just this kind of situation. The Temple authorities were disturbed that Peter and the other disciples continued to preach in the Temple though they had been commanded not to do so. "Didn't we command you not to teach in the name of Jesus?" they asked Peter. They were the authorities. They thought they deserved obedience, and could not get over the fact the Christians were rebelling against their directives. Peter explained why: "We ought to obey God rather than men" (Acts 5:29). Peter was telling the Temple authorities that their power was valid only when consistent with the commands of God. And if it came to a choice between the two, Peter would go to the very Source of authority— God!

Societies always pay for bad leadership. Sometimes people inherit the bad leadership *they didn't pray for*. That was what had happened to Israel when Hosea wrote these words: "Israel hath cast off the thing that is good: the enemy shall pursue him. They have set up kings, *but not by me;* they have made princes, *and I knew it not....* They have sown the wind, and they shall reap the whirlwind" (Hosea 8:3-7, italics added). Israel's political tragedy was the result of the rulership of kings and princes who had no power base in God. Hence, they

31

had no real authority. And all Israel would suffer.

The United States and other nations in the twentieth century are no different. Their ground of authority is *still* God. And that makes Christian ministry in Washington and other world power centers imperative!

CHAPTER III

Warfare In Pajamas

Sometimes while on the White House staff I felt like a person who had just been placed before the controls of a Boeing 747, *in flight,* without ever having been in an airplane cockpit before! Those were the times when I felt truly unprepared to be where I was. To shift metaphors, I felt like a warrior who had shown up for hand-to-hand combat wearing pajamas.

We saw in the last chapter that the base of the government official's power is God. This means that his battle dress must be the armor of Christ. Much bad government is caused by governing officials who have not understood that their work is spiritual in nature and that they must therefore be properly attired!

Paul closes out Romans 13 with words apparently comprising a hymn. And if it is music, Romans 13:11-14 is no less than a reveille:

... now it is high time to awake out of sleep: for

now is our salvation nearer than when we believed. The night is far spent, the day is at hand: let us therefore cast off the works of darkness, and let us put on the armour of light. Let us walk honestly, as in the day; not in rioting and drunkenness, not in chambering and wantonness, not in strife and envying. But put ye on the Lord Jesus Christ, and make not provision for the flesh, to fulfill the lusts thereof.

There can be no doubt that Paul winds up his discourse on authority and civil power with fighting words; a battle motif is struck! Why? That is answered in Ephesians 6:

Finally, my brethren, be strong in the Lord, and in the power of his might. Put on the whole armour of God, that ye may be able to stand against the wiles of the devil. For we wrestle not against flesh and blood, but against principalities, against powers, against the rulers of the darkness of the world, against spiritual wickedness in high places [10-12].

God has established human authorities to wage the battle against the forces of chaos, lawlessness and brokenness. And the stress of Ephesians 6 is that this is *spiritual* warfare. But tragically, this is the kind of warfare for which civil authorities seem least prepared! They are ready for economic conflict, political battles, military confrontation, but not for the spiritual warfare which underlies all the others!

Paul thus sounds a reveille to Christians today to wake up to the needs of reaching the government authority with the claims of Christ. It is imperative because, says Paul, the time of judgment is at hand.

Warfare in Pajamas

There is an immediacy to this judgment we do not always understand. Judgment is not limited to the time we stand before God in eternity. The immediate judgment of an army or athletic team begins every time a battle or contest must be faced. If the Los Angeles Rams take on the Oakland Raiders without making preparation, their judgment begins with the kickoff. So it is with nations and governments. Senator Mark Hatfield, in his book, *Conflict and Conscience,* says this:

> The history of Israel teaches us ... [that] the people could turn to God for relief from an oppressive and evil ruler.... But we should also be aware that Israel frequently suffered under oppressive rulers as a direct result of its own evil conduct and disobedience to God's commandments. In other words, corrupt and evil government resulted from the moral degeneration of the people themselves [p. 151].

Such was the immediacy of judgment in which God gave up Israel to the consequences of her actions (see Romans 1). Perhaps this was the kind of accounting Paul had in mind in Romans 13:4: "... if thou do that which is evil, be afraid, for he [the ruling authority] ... is the minister of God, a revenger to execute wrath upon him that doeth evil."

There can be no doubt that God is speaking to nations today, in immediate judgment. His voice is thundering with warning in Watergate, in governmental mismanagement of national resources, in authorities leading their societies in moral confusion, in the arms race...

Can we not hear the accents of judgment in the fact that nations annually spend $12,330 to arm a soldier and $219 to educate a child (from *World Military and Social Expenditures 1976*)? Professor Thomas Schelling of Harvard, in *The Christian Science Monitor,* said that "A reasoned evaluation of where we may be in 25 years suggests that we will not be able to regulate nuclear weapons around the world in 1999 any better than we can control the 'Saturday night special,' heroin, or pornography today" (November 18, 1975).

The agents for God's immediate judgment are at hand. All He has to do is give us up to the consequences of our own refusal to follow Him, as government leaders and common citizens!

But the immediate judgment of God can be corrective. We can have a positive attitude about this level of judgment if we see it as we do a stop signal at a railroad crossing. We may be troubled that we are slowed down by the blinking signal; but we can be grateful that it warned us not to proceed as we were. This is why Paul summons us to wake up in light of the coming judgment. We can still do something about government and leadership not resting itself on God nor dressing itself in the armor of Christ.

For there is also eternal judgment. In the next chapter, we will note how God holds accountable those to whom He gives responsibility. Government leaders who have been gifted by God with leadership will stand before God in eternity as sure as will the least citizen!

But the Holy Spirit, through Paul, gives us a much more compelling reason to wake up to good citizenship and leadership under the sovereignty of God: We should wake up because the day of opportunity is at hand!

While I was living in Washington, I occasionally had the chance to worship with the Dallas Cowboys when they would come to town to play the Washington Redskins. Billy Zeoli, the Cowboys' chaplain, would host guests for the service, which would be at the motel where the football team was housed. I remember one occasion when the Dallas team was in Washington to play the Redskins for the league championship. On that morning I arrived early, sat down beside then-Congressman Gerald Ford and began conversing with him. But when the players began arriving, Ford and I forgot our conversation. The men entering the room looked like raging bulls someone had penned up. Their day of opportunity had arrived, and they were ready to take on their opponents!

God's servants in society should approach their contests with the same eagerness. The government leader should submit himself to God because the Lord has placed a tremendous opportunity before him. Chairman Mao admonished his cadres to "seize the time." But this is the mandate, the command, that God places before those who are gifted with authority: Seize the day of opportunity to overcome the enemies of God's system of order!

To do that, citizens and leaders alike are going to have to throw off the flimsy garments of night: "Let us therefore cast off the works of darkness and let us put on the armour of light" (Romans 13:12b). In other words, says Paul, the uniform for the day is battle dress.

The Apostle catalogs for us the kind of night garments that will not do for the challenge of today. They include the nightclothes of "revelry and drunkenness." By "revelry," he means attitudes and actions that disturb others and debase the person doing the disturbing. This involves the loss of respect for oneself and distrust from others.

The Apostle Paul may never have heard of a Washington cocktail party, but he scored a direct hit when, under the Holy Spirit's inspiration, he included drunkenness in his list of unworthy nightclothes. If Americans really understood the scope of the alcohol problem in Washington, they would be terrified. At White House parties, one would scarcely finish one drink before an usher was at his elbow offering another. Sometimes White House aides would leave the party in one part of the building to go to their offices in another part of the building where they would make or implement decisions with minds clouded by the alcohol they had just consumed!

Outside the White House, the American public has been exposed to congressmen who have been stopped for drunk driving and chairmen of major House committees whose wild escapades with prostitutes have cost them their leadership roles. And all the while the uniform of the day is battle dress, not the nightclothes of drunkenness and revelry!

Paul further lists as flimsy sleeping garments "immorality and shamelessness." The words in the King James Version of the Bible are "chambering" and "wantonness." "Chambering" is a lifestyle pursued by someone who has no idea of moral guidelines. He does what he wants to do, when he wishes to do it. "Wantonness" is the spirit of that person so tangled in lust that he does not care who sees him do anything.

Again the Holy Spirit is painfully on target. For this, after all, is the age when one of the most powerful men in Congress disgraced himself with a nightclub stripper. It is the time when another lost his position of power because of wanton immorality with a member of his staff. When the dawn of battle blazed with intense, exposing light, it was clear they were caught in their nightclothes and not dressed in their armor!

"Contention and envy" are included in Paul's list of unfit garments. "Strife" or "contention" comes when a person permits his hunger for prestige and position to become the central desire of his life. Morality, truth, honesty are all secondary to getting or maintaining that place of power. Perhaps no other sin is more to blame for the scandals of the Watergate period than this overwhelming desire to hold on to the presidency at any price. And the political polarization which paralyzes so many governments is a result of this contentious spirit!

But "envy" is behind such contention. In a period when Americans ought to be united against common foes, they are often split, with one interest group torn in envy against another. As long as envy drives would-be warriors for God's Kingdom to war with one another, they are blinded to the real enemy who has already entered the gates. Contention and envy become the flimsy garments of darkness which are not fit for the rigors of battle!

Our leaders and citizens alike must get themselves dressed out for battle. "Put on the Lord Jesus Christ," Paul urges in Romans 13:14. The picture reaches all the way back to Eden when an exposed humanity tried to cover itself with leaves. God saw that covering would not do for the chill night of sin brought on when man severed himself from God. So God provided a covering. And that has been the way of God's work ever since—to cloak humanity in Christ's conquest of sin and death.

That is the only armor fitting for the nature of warfare that the human race faces against Satan, its common enemy. If the war is one against arrows, one dresses in a knight's armor; if the contest is with a tank, one had better be covered by another tank. And if we are going to war against spiritual powers, we must be clothed with Christ's righteousness.

If all this is true—and history proves it is—then Christians everywhere must be seized by the urgency of presenting Christ to government officials. For multitudes of them are in the front-line trenches, eyeball to eyeball with the enemy, yet they are there in their pajamas because they have not put on the armor of Christ!

CHAPTER IV

The Two Revolutions

What happens when governments do not see that their authority is a gift from God? What happens when leaders of nations do not grasp the importance of meeting their challenges dressed properly? The answers are graphically illustrated in the eighteenth century.

The American Revolution spawned a century of political storms. The French Revolution boiled and churned over France almost before the winds in America had died down.

But there were vast differences between the two revolutions. One purported to exalt humanity to godhood, but reduced it to a faceless mass mob in a raving reign of terror. The other revolution faced frankly the limitations of man but extended to humanity a dignity not achieved in any other political system. One revolution plopped its people into the lap of a dictator. The other revolution brought into being a system of bloodless, orderly revolutions of

41

the electorate every four years. One revolution burned brightly, then fizzled within a decade. The other moves into its third century.

Reasons for these differences were summed up quite well by the Erie *Times-News,* in an editorial on July 3, 1976:

> A tough realism, born of an ancient Biblical idea, underlays the founding of the U.S.—a conviction that human beings, including the most elevated statesmen of Government, can go wrong. They were regarded, in Scriptural terms, as subject to sin....
>
> The American Revolution came shortly before another one in Europe, the French Revolution of 1789 ... the basic difference cited (by scholars) involved the French "optimism" about human direction vs. American "pessimism." The mostly Protestant early Americans were sharply conscious of human fallibility—their perverse vulnerability to sin. The implication was that society should not put full or final power over peoples' lives in the hands of any human sovereign or group, no matter how learned or illustrious; they were prey to corruption.... It is a system of restricted powers, of reserved areas of action, possibly the only Government in the world in which no human entity is given sovereign authority.

It would be wrong to assume that all our forefathers were deeply committed evangelical Christians. They were not. But as we saw in an earlier chapter, biblical principles made up the underlying philosophy of the kind of society we would become.

The crisis today is that there are once again two revolutionary alternatives in the world. One is the option of a system based on belief in the sovereignty and transcendence of God—a system of responsible freedom. The other alternative is a system based on human messiahs and totalitarianism.

If leaders in the Western democracies, especially the United States, do not understand the importance and foundational role of the spiritual dimension in their personal lives and institutions, then freedom will disappear from the planet!

We can see this in the unfolding histories these two revolutionary systems have already written for themselves.

For example, the system based on God assumes great goals for man; the system based on humanism assumes—oddly enough—great goals for the state. The difference is in the views of the systems about the nature of man.

The political authority under God bases its philosophy of man on the Bible. Here is what the Bible teaches about man:

- he is created in the image of God;
- even when man freely violates this image he is precious enough that God gives Himself to restore man to wholeness;
- thus the Bible sees man as having the potential for redemption;
- even the lowliest person is of infinite value in the eyes of God;
- every human being can become the vessel of God, and hence be capable of godlike works, through the Holy Spirit;

> • despite the fact we have rejected God and crucified His Son, He is reserving a place in His realm and is coming back for all who accept His provision!

The Christian faith has been accused of propagating a low view of man because of its stress on the doctrine of sin. But to the contrary, there is no higher view of man anywhere. The very reason for Christianity's talk of sin is to announce the Good News that sin can be forgiven!

Now look at the political principles which come from the Bible's lofty philosophy of man. Basically, since man is created in the image of God, he should be free to make his own choices. People are "endowed by their Creator with certain inalienable rights," to use the language of the founding fathers. People are given the right to life, liberty and the pursuit of happiness because they are made in the image of God. That means responsible freedom.

Further, since man is worth something, he is entitled to the protection of the law. The Bible has already spoken of humanity's worth. God died for mankind—there can be no greater worth than that! Certainly, then, the laws are made for the protection of this precious creature. But there is another implication. Since man is capable of good works—God, after all, considers him redeemable—man is therefore responsible before the law.

However, in a system without God, without the Bible, there is a great difference in the definition of man. And the political implications are tragic! Our Declaration of Independence, for example, says that

"... whenever any Form of Government becomes destructive of these Ends [the right to life, liberty and the pursuit of happiness], it is the right of the people to alter or abolish it." But in a totalitarian system without God, it is the *people* who are abolished when they are in conflict with the state, and not the governing power. In the Russia of 1917, Lenin labeled dissidents who threatened the new power of the Marxist establishment, as "harmful insects" who needed to be purged from the land. Calling a human being a "harmful insect" is a long slide from the Bible's high view of man. Not surprisingly, the implementation of Lenin's philosophy resulted in the infamous concentration camp network Aleksandr Solzhenitsyn chronicles in *The Gulag Archipelago*.

There is a crooked line of illogic which produces such abominations. Since the system without God has no precise definition of man, it makes up its own. The state becomes the absolute. Since it is the highest entity in the society, nothing can be done to imperil the state, and thus there is no place for dissent. Further, human life is not of infinite worth in such a system. Therefore, if an individual gets in the way of the state and its goals, that human life may be purged. Hitler, needing an enemy to arouse the German fighting spirit and consolidate his own power, assaulted the Jews. Ho Chi Minh found individual land owners in North Vietnam stood in the way of his goals. He had them killed—like Stalin and Mao had done before him. It really makes no difference whether the state is rightist or leftist when it comes to systems without God; either way the result is disastrous.

During the Chinese cultural revolution, the wife of Liu Shao-chi was brought to trial. She cried, "as a Chinese woman, as a Chinese woman communist, I am independent." To which her interrogator responded, "you are a class reject."

So it is in a system not under the sovereignty of God. Human beings have no worth, and are subject to the highly relative definitions of whoever holds power at the time. The Russian communists prior to 1922 did not even carry out their prosecutions under law, for none existed. "Only a revolutionary sense of justice (always infallible) guided those doing the purging" (Solzhenitsyn, *Gulag Archipelago,* p. 32).

There is another difference between governments which rest ultimately on God and those which do not. The authority under God believes there is objective right and wrong to which even governments must adhere. The power without God really holds that right and wrong are determined by the authorities in place at the moment.

The governing system resting itself on God recognizes the law of God as the base for all just law. It holds that a law is right when it conforms to the law of God. The Scripture is the authority for such a position: "The law of the Lord is perfect, converting the soul: the testimony of the Lord is sure, making wise the simple. The statutes of the Lord are right, rejoicing the heart: the commandment of the Lord is pure, enlightening the eyes" (Psalm 19:7-8). Further, Jesus said, "Think not that I am come to

46

destroy the law, or the prophets: I am not come to destroy, but to fulfill'' (Matthew 5:17).

On the other hand, a system with a strictly humanist base has no such absolute for right, and the consequences on the citizen are disastrous. Soviet dissident, Andre Amalrik, points this out:

> Evidently we have reached the point where the idea of power is no longer connected with either a doctrine, the personality of a leader or a tradition, but only with power itself.... Good is what at any moment is required by authority. Naturally, such a morality ... has totally demoralized society [*Will The Soviet Union Survive Until 1984?*, pp. 22, 37].

A third difference between a government based on God's precepts and one that rests on itself is this: In the former, there is the knowledge that ruling powers are ordained of God, and are thus accountable to Him; in the latter, the ruling elites are accountable only to their requirements for survival.

As we have seen, the Source of authority is God. Romans 13 does not mean that God approves of every ruler. What it does stress is that God is the base of just authority anywhere. Americans—and the world—saw how this philosophy works in practice during the Watergate episode. The President of the United States, in the minds of many, violated the integrity of his office. And not even the President was above the law or morality. Therefore he had to give up that office. He was accountable to something beyond the dictates of his holding power. The President was answerable to decency and honesty and truth. Those matters stem from God's law, not man's!

But in a godless system, the rulers do not see themselves ultimately accountable to either God or the people. Mao tried to say that the people were his final guide, the "god" of China. But Mao was the ruler, and he determined even who the people were. To suggest that the people are the judges is heresy in a system with no absolutes, for that would imply that the individual is more important than the state.

Since the ruling elites recognize no ultimate accountability in a godless state, they decide that the people are incapable of making decisions for themselves. Thus the rulers determine the survival needs, and that becomes morality.

Finally, the system based on God rests on a foundational philosophy that history is going somewhere. But in godless states, survival becomes the only real objective of history.

The governing power looking to God for its authority must confront the Christian view that history is going somewhere. The Bible teaches that history is moving *toward judgment—accountability*: "And as it is appointed unto men once to die, but after this the judgment" (Hebrews 9:27). Also, the Bible shows that history is moving *toward resurrection—a new order*: "But now is Christ risen from the dead, and become the firstfruits of them that slept.... For as in Adam all die, even so in Christ shall all be made alive" (I Corinthians 15:20-22). Then, the Bible reveals that history is moving *towards heaven—a new Kingdom*: "And I saw a new heaven and a new earth ... And I John saw the holy city, new Jerusalem, coming down from God out of heaven" (Revelation 21:1, 2). The Bible teaches that there is infinitely greater significance to history than mere survival. Any system which says it is based on God's order must confront that basic teaching.

However, the governing power without God views history merely as a struggle for survival. This robs history of its Lord. One of Marxism's most glaring errors is its false conception of history. Marxism borrows Hegel's dialectic to dress up its doctrine. But it never deals with the fact that what it is really saying, then, is that history has a plan without a Planner!

Further, power without God robs history of its integrity. In Marxism, history is no longer the crucible in which God and humanity interract, but a mere concoction of blind and amoral forces which nevertheless are going somewhere!

Marxism robs history of its beauty. For if the only purpose of humanity's trek across time is survival, then only the strong have a place in the world. There is no room for the manger, for the cross, for the Jesus who gives sight to the blind!

Up to the present, America has stoutly resisted tyranny, but that is no reason for complacency. For there is no guarantee that just because a society began with the ideals of God, it will continue. States and governing systems can cut themselves off from their roots until those roots die. It is time for Christians to ask if that is happening in America.

There are some frightening evidences that we are leaving the solid mooring of God's philosophies and drifting into the sea of moral and political anarchy. The gauge of this is the increasing preoccupation of American society with violence. A continuing bloodbath spills out into the dens of millions of American homes from television. Violence is anti-life and proceeds from a low view of life. This contradicts the biblical view of humanity which produces structures of responsible freedom. Today this philosophy is being displaced.

Another cause for concern for Christians is the fact that many are satisfied to go through the motions of some cultural religion without genuine and deep commitment to God. Politicians and commentators mouth the words of God without really following through in lifestyle. As Francis Schaeffer has pointed out, we live on the memory of religious traditions without the living experience of God. We must not be "religious" just for the sake of preserving our society, or he will say to us, as He did to ancient Israel, "I hate your sacrifices."

For the truth is that a people whose only commitment is to a religious system for the sake of their own survival are little different in actual behavior from those with no religious loyalties at all!

Jesus said, however, that His followers would be the salt of the earth. Salt not only flavors, it also preserves. The Bible is full of evidence that God is always looking to a committed minority to serve as the preservative of a society. He probed Sodom and Gomorrah. He searched the world in the day of

Noah for a righteous man, and He preserved the human race because of Noah's faith. Now, in the twentieth century with its capabilities for overkill, and in the darkness of its creeping madness, God is still looking to His disciples for the preservation of civilization and ordered society.

Some years ago, a friend of mine was in a certain totalitarian nation. Through a series of what appeared to be coincidences, he met an official of that government. My friend discovered that the man was an underground Christian. As their conversation highlighted the official's Christian commitment, he became nervous, fearing he might be bugged. He suggested to my friend that they go to a certain lake and rent a boat, row to the middle, and have their discussion without fear of listening devices.

When they were a safe distance from land, the official began talking about his position in the government. My friend responded, "Sir, God needs a man in this nation's government."

The man quickly replied, "Then I am that man!"

The United States is no different. God needs His people in positions of leadership, be they liberal or conservative, Democrat or Republican. The very nature of this society hinges on a continuing commitment to the truth of God.

Those who minister in Washington and other capitals are winning individuals to Christ—but they are also contributing to the total life of the society.

We shall turn now to look at some of these "missionaries to the mighty," at their work and its impact.

51

PART II
Missionaries to the Mighty

CHAPTER V

Bacon, Eggs and Prayer

The President of the United States was going to a prayer meeting. So said his schedule sheet, so read the White House press corps.

Most of the reporters knew that the prayer meeting would be a breakfast at the Washington Hilton Hotel. They would have to rise early and slice through the downtown Washington traffic, by then at its peak for the morning.

Across a small street from the White House West Wing, a group assembled in a conference room in the Old Executive Office Building. The appearance of the ancient gray structure prompted chuckles or awe, depending on one's point of view. To some, it seemed a dour mountain of concrete doodads, piled one on another at random. To others, the building was a persistent statement of the Victorian sense of the imposing nature of authority. Some of the door-knobs inside still bore the engraved seals of the military groups housed there when the Old Executive Office Building was the home of the War Department. Now, however, the structure sheltered a strategy session on moving the President from the White House to the Washington Hilton.

Sitting around a large conference table were representatives of the Secret Service, members of the President's scheduling team, an advance man, and a representative of another Christian fellowship that assists with details of the National Prayer Breakfast—sometimes called the "Presidential Prayer Breakfast." Officially, the breakfast is sponsored by a committee from the House and Senate.

The men now verbally rehearsed getting the President to the prayer breakfast. Precisely at 7 a.m., he would walk through the White House Diplomatic Reception Room, down the canopied sidewalk to his limousine, parked on the south lawn. Secret Service cars would be placed before and after the President's car. A phalanx of Washington motorcycle police would lead the caravan through the morning traffic.

At 7:15 a.m., the President would proceed to a "holding room" in the Washington Hilton, where he would spend a few moments with members of his Cabinet, the Supreme Court, the Joint Chiefs, congressional leadership and an assortment of other dignitaries, including some from the diplomatic corps.

The President, at 7:30 a.m., would advance to the dais on the huge stage of the main ballroom of the hotel. There, he would breakfast with yet more dignitaries. The President would be among the speakers, though he would not deliver the main address.

On this particular morning, as the President walked onstage, he was greeted by 3,000 people who had come to share the prayer meeting from all over the United States and the world. There were 285 people present from the Legislative Branch of the government. The Executive Branch counted 120 of its people at the breakfast. Included from the Judicial Branch and the military were another 150. Ninety members of the diplomatic corps were present, including Soviet Ambassador Anatoly Dobrynin and the Mayor of Moscow. Twenty-five United Nations ambassadors had come down from New York City.

From across the United States there were 10 governors and lieutenant governors, 30 members of state legislatures, 35 attorneys general, 50 mayors. Additionally, there were 50 leaders of the petroleum industry, 100 representatives of the American banking and business communities, 135 educators, 50 from the medical profession. Fifteen athletes, 35 executives of service organizations and 35 religious leaders shared the breakfast. Pat Boone was there, as was Billy Graham.

Red-frocked waiters and waitresses scurried over the ballroom serving the 3,000 guests. This year, the participants were not served the usual fare of quiche Lorraine, bulging sausages and sweet rolls. The meal was a meager offering of what the world's poor usually eat for breakfast.

Oregon's Senator Mark Hatfield was the primary speaker of the morning. Recalling the "inaugural" message of Jesus, in which He declared it was His intention to "announce good news to the poor," Hatfield told the audience:

> Today, our abundance, which has brought material blessings to so many, threatens us spiritually as a peril. Never have we known such wealth, but never have we worshipped wealth more.... Whereas people once looked toward God for salvation, our culture now propels their daily lives toward the domination of nature and fellow human beings in ceaseless quest for material accumulation.... From such bondage Jesus Christ yearns to set us free.... Our materialism holds us in bondage to what we consume and possess. But Christ's good news sets us free from the poverty of abundance.

Hatfield's remarks were followed by a period of silent prayer. Then the President of the United States, his Cabinet, members of the Congress, the Judicial Branch and officers of the Pentagon, their medallions glinting in the bright lights, filed from the ballroom and into the Washington day.

For some of them, globe-girdling activities would be handled with a renewed sense of values. For others, there would be an increasing awareness that even their ponderous authority would have to be subject to an even higher Authority if it would be authentic. And for some, the prayer breakfast would have been just another ritual of their own private religion—that of the secular temples of Washington.

Some of those who attended the prayer breakfast had actually begun their involvement the night before. Dinners and discussion groups assembled all over the Washington Hilton, as Christians from around the world compared notes, prayed for one another and discovered new ways of reaching more leaders for Christ.

Late in the evening before the prayer breakfast, John Staggers had hosted a group of black Americans in a penthouse suite high above the Washington streets. Staggers, a black man himself and former aide to Mayor Walter Washington of the District of Columbia, was now on the staff of the Fellowship Foundation. He concentrated his work on the black community and urban strategies, especially within Washington. Some of his guests that night were Christians, others were not. Lively debate went on as Staggers presented his own testimony for Christ.

His meeting was typical of others in session. Elsewhere, Indian leaders were gathering to talk about Christ, judges and members of the legal profession were in prayer groups, as were many other special groups. Many of them would be in such sessions through the following afternoon.

The events related to the National Prayer Breakfast are one aspect of the work of Christians in Washington. The Fellowship Foundation is another facet of that work. It would be impossible to catalog all the ministries of this group outside Washington. They range from Chuck Colson's prison ministries to programs of outreach to golf professionals. Through it all, the fellowship as an institution tries to stay as invisible as possible. It prefers to be the catalyst rather than a sustaining institution.

But there can be no doubt that the National Prayer Breakfast is the most visible of the fellowship's undertakings.

It all started with a chance meeting between then-Kansas Senator Frank Carlson and Conrad Hilton, the hotel owner. Hilton had come to Kansas City for visits with Dwight Eisenhower, who was there preparing for his presidential campaign. As Hilton came out of the meeting with Ike, Carlson mentioned an impending visit with Billy Graham. The talk turned to religion.

"Senator," said Hilton, "anytime I can be of help in a cause for Christ, you call on me."

The offer was forgotten until after the election of Eisenhower. A group of senators had been meeting for prayer for some time, and it occurred to Carlson that Ike might like to attend a session. "I'd be delighted," responded the President-elect.

Carlson recalls the rest:

> We met in the Vandenberg Room in the Senate, which holds about 35 people. The House had a prayer breakfast group, and they wanted in on the meeting too, if we had the President with us. I was really in trouble. I had invited the President! What should I do?
>
> My mind flashed back to that meeting in June with Conrad Hilton. I picked up the phone and called him in Beverly Hills and said, "Conrad, you made a commitment to me last June. We want to have a prayer breakfast with the President of the United States. I want you to let us use the ballroom of the Mayflower Hotel, and I want you to pick up the tab."

So, in February, 1953, Hilton supplied the ballroom and the funds. The prayer breakfast movement was on its way.

But the idea had been born and began much earlier by the founder of the Fellowship Foundation, Abram Vereide. An immigrant from Norway, Vereide was a Methodist minister who developed a special burden for reaching leaders in every walk of life. "The great demand everywhere is for men of the highest order with a consecrated head, heart and hand," preached Vereide.

In the mid-thirties, Vereide was living in Seattle. He was increasingly disturbed about the spiritual condition of the United States—especially that of officialdom. He would discuss his concerns with businessman Walter Douglas. One day, Douglas suggested that Vereide should target his ministry at men like Douglas himself.

Soon Vereide had brought together several Seattle leaders for Bible study and prayer. They would share at breakfast meetings, studying the Bible and praying together. Then, in 1939, one of the group was elected Governor of Washington. Vereide went to work organizing a prayer breakfast for him, and some 300 leaders were in attendance. The seed was planted and began to sprout. After moving to Chicago in 1943, Vereide organized leadership groups centered around Christ.

In 1942, the residence where Vereide would convene groups in Washington was sold, and he began looking for a permanent home for his Washington ministries. A beautiful house near the Shoreham

Hotel was located, and after some tight financial maneuvers, Vereide began his work there.

Vereide died in 1969. But his work continues to bear fruit. His successor was a young Oregonian by the name of Doug Coe. He moves through the Washington powerhouses with the same ease and determination to minister as did Vereide. The ICL designation has been dropped, and the group is now called, simply, the fellowship. Dropping the institutional title was done in the hope it would stress the philosophy of fellowship rather than organization.

Thus these brothers and companions in Christ do not consider themselves to be in an organization, but in a state of fellowship with one another. The spirit of that fellowship, they feel, is described in I John 1:3:

> "That which we have seen and heard declare we unto you, that ye also may have fellowship with us: and truly our fellowship is with the Father, and with his Son Jesus Christ."

Some in the fellowship even desire to avoid using the word "Christian" to characterize themselves. They prefer to be designated as followers of Jesus Christ. The term "Christian," they say, was never used by Jesus. They feel it has become a divisive word in the light of their work, and that to be termed followers of Christ sounds dynamic rather than institutional, like "Christian." The Reformation, believes Doug Coe, shifted the stress of the Christian life from working for God to knowing God. If one centers on knowing God through following and learning of Christ, the work for God will follow.

"We discovered it was necessary to actually do away with the corporation itself before we could convince others—and ourselves—that we are in fact committed to simply relating on a fellowship basis with men in the spirit of Christ," said Clifton Robinson, a worker with the fellowship.

The aim of the fellowship is stated simply: "... to know God through Christ and to love Him with all our heart, and with all of our soul, and with all our mind, and with all of our strength and to love fellow men as ourselves."

Several objectives are listed to help reach the overall goal:

- Encourage a fellowship of responsible men banded together to find through Christ a better way of everyday living, in order to promote for home, community, nation, the world, and at every level of society a leadership led by God;

- Work together to encourage a spiritual awakening throughout the world through prayer, discussion and fellowship;

- Encourage men around the world towards more effective leadership in the areas of their own life pursuits;

- Commit ourselves daily through the power of Christ to being and building bridges of communication and understanding between people.

Many times I saw firsthand how these objectives came to life. I had learned in my acquaintance with Doug Coe to keep my passport updated. One week I traveled to London to speak at a conference put together by Wallace Haines, the fellowship's resident man in Europe, and an early associate of Abram Vereide.

Haines had arranged for me to meet in London the Viscount Caldecote, a British industrialist. Together we would drive up to Windsor, where the conference would be held.

When I got there, I began to see the scope of the fellowship's involvement with men everywhere. Present were people like a member of the parliament of Northern Ireland, a bank executive from Paris, an international vice president of the Jaycees, from Barcelona, a Greek student, then in exile, an engineer from Belgium. For three days, some 25 of us lived together, ate together, studied together, prayed together. Though we were so diverse, Christ had welded us into a sharing unit.

Again I saw this work of building constructive relationships between people on a trip with Coe to Costa Rica. There we shared with the President of the country and a prayer group consisting of many of the nation's politicians and businessmen.

Leadership groups have been established or other types of work undertaken in Ethiopia, Chad, the Ivory Coast, Kenya, Ghana, Egypt, India, Indonesia, Japan, South Korea, the Philippines, Australia, and virtually all the countries of Central America and Europe.

In the United States, the fellowship was helped establish Governor's Prayer Breakfasts in 47 states. There have been some 1,000 Prayer Breakfasts sponsored by mayors. One-third of the states have leadership groups in their legislatures. Additionally, the fellowship sparks leadership sharing groups within organizations like the Jaycees, the American Medical Association, Kiwanis, American Banking Association and others.

The fellowship does not come into organizations as an institution from the outside. Rather, men within the organizations who are also part of the fellowship will encourage their peers to meet together.

This is what men in the fellowship mean when they talk of "building relationships." As individuals get to know each other, much of their gathering becomes spontaneous, making an ideal context for the formation of a leadership group or development of a prayer breakfast.

Sometimes such "relationship building" will happen at a dinner table at Fellowship House. I recall one evening shortly before the death of David Lawrence, the noted journalist. Though he was Jewish, Lawrence had been instrumental in helping start prayer groups on Capitol Hill—which we will discuss in the next chapter. Doug Coe decided that he wanted to pull together a small group to share in the spirit of Christ's love with Lawrence. So that night there gathered at the table with David Lawrence two White House aides, the director of the United States Information Agency, several members of Congress and retired military personnel. One by one we went around the table that evening telling David Lawrence why we appreciated him, always stressing that it was in the spirit of Christ that we shared such love.

The Fellowship Foundation has often been a target for criticism. Sometimes it is accused of being too nebulous, but that very obscurity makes it a hard mark to hit. The fellowship has been criticized for lacking cogent doctrine and for too little emphasis on Christ and the need for salvation. However, Abram Vereide was a deeply committed follower of Christ, as is Doug Coe. And the fellowship adheres to Scripture more closely than its critics realize.

Another criticism has been that the fellowship is too limited. It is claimed that not enough effort is made to include women and minorities in its ministries. There is, however, an active set of projects designed to minister to women, under the leadership of Barbara Priddy, a member of the fellowship staff. The fellowship may need to think beyond just having special groups for women, however, and begin including women executives more in the larger meetings of male leadership.

There are now groups for wives of Congressmen, Diplomats and Cabinet members. And there is always a women's leadership seminar as part of the National Prayer Breakfast.

The fellowship continues to stress diversification. Adopting Chuck Colson's prison ministry under the Fellowship House roof has widened that diversification. As Colson chronicles it in his book, *Born Again,* his brief stay in prison during the Watergate affair led to a hunger to establish ministries in prisons.

Members of the fellowship had moved around

Colson rapidly after his conversion became public knowledge and continued "discipling" Colson through his own stay in jail. It was natural, then, for Colson to use the fellowship's model for the pattern of work among inmates. The goal of Colson's work has been to establish leadership groups behind the walls of institutions. Like the fellowship's ministry in government, business and service organizations, Colson enlists inmates themselves who are Christian to begin work with their peers.

Through an arrangement with the Federal Bureau of Prisons, Colson has been permitted to bring prisoners eligible for furlough to Fellowship House for two weeks of concentrated training on leadership. When the inmates return to their institutions, they come trained to set up small groups for Bible study and prayer sharing.

Finding the prisoners to bring to Washington was a major undertaking. Colson enlisted the assistance of "friends of the fellowship" in the various regions of the country. They came to Washington and were trained. On returning to their regions, these "friends" were introduced to wardens and chaplains at Federal prison facilities. For two or three days, Colson's helpers would interview inmates, looking for those with Christian commitment and leadership ability. These would then be brought to Washington.

The fellowship rarely makes intensive financial appeals. Usually, money needs are cared for by people in the "core," those most intimately involved in being the catalysts behind the fellowship.

And since the fellowship moves by the motivation of its people, there is no heavy program planning. The few staffers and many "friends of the fellowship" create and innovate much of the work themselves. Spontaneity is not always the norm, but the fellowship believes that if people are involved in a close relationship to Christ, they will spark relational ministries to others. And that, generally, is **exactly** what happens.

CHAPTER VI

The Prayer Network

The White House, during the period I worked there, had a resident Santa Claus. His name was John Nidecker. John was a fellow best described as a "generalist," which meant his skills ranged from congressional relations to donning himself in a white beard and red suit at Christmas time and ho-hoing at the staff Christmas party. Santa Claus was an appropriate symbol for John, because he gave the White House of those days a gift much more precious than sparkling packages. He is one who gave leadership in a very important project.

One afternoon, my boss, Harry Dent, asked if I would meet him and Nidecker the following morning for breakfast in the staff mess. John and aide Richard Burriss had an idea they wanted to discuss with us, Harry explained.

Before seven the next morning, I was waving at the guards as I entered the Southwest Gate. I met in the dining room with Burriss, Dent and Nidecker.

For some time, Nidecker and Burriss had wanted to get members of the staff together for prayer on a regular basis. The idea had been suggested by David Lawrence, who was active in a group on Capitol Hill. Nidecker wanted Dent and me to join with him in sparking interest within the White House. I agreed to serve as a contact person for the effort. A time was set for our regular breakfast meetings.

The next week, I circulated a memorandum to some of my colleagues I thought might be interested. We would meet that Thursday, I told them, at 7 a.m. in the West Wing Executive Dining Room. The day came with a half-dozen or so present. After eating we went around the table asking the men for prayer requests. Several of the staffers prayed, and we dismissed.

Soon the loose structure of simply eating and praying was expanded. Each week a different person would be responsible for a Bible study or devotional thought. But the period of prayer remained the focal point of the meetings. We would always stand and link hands. It might have appeared awkward for men who were supposed to have the reputation for political toughness to grasp hands, but that act enabled us to affirm our oneness in Christ. And it broke down the inhibitions of staff hierarchy. In rank, I was probably the lowest man in the room. But I did not think of that as I linked hands in prayer with men who bore the title, "Special Counsel to the President."

Generally, as with many of the prayer cells in Washington, we did not have many visitors. But occasionally some interesting folk would drop in. One day the entertainer, Sammy Davis, Jr., was visiting Bob Brown, a regular in the prayer group. That day Brown was bringing the devotional and asked Davis to accompany him to the breakfast. Davis was amazed when he was invited to stand and link hands with members of the White House staff while we prayed for him and one another.

On another day the acting chief of state from Cambodia was present with his staff. That morning several Cabinet officers were invited to meet with us. Secretary of State William Rogers attended along with Secretary of Housing and Urban Development George Romney, who was one of the speakers. The Cambodians were Buddhist, but the remarks were centered on Christ. Many of us hoped the experience would be a positive witness to the Cambodians.

Probably the most memorable White House staff breakfast I attended was my last one. It was shortly after the inauguration of President Nixon to his second term. Richard Burriss suggested it would be a good idea to launch the new period of our work in a spirit of prayer and commitment. Billy Graham was asked to speak. The room was filled to its capacity of about 30.

I had been in charge of arrangements. A bit on the nervous side, I arrived early to make sure all was in order. John Erlichman had established the habit of meeting each morning with a member of his staff and going over the day's schedule over breakfast. Erlichman always had his meeting in the Executive

Dining Room. As I barged into the room that morning, there sat Erlichman and his staff man. I knew that in a few moments the guests would begin arriving. It was obvious Erlichman was not there for the prayer meeting—though he was invited. He and his aide were already eating their breakfast. I also knew that I was far too low on the totem pole to tell John Erlichman he would have to clear the room. It was just as certain he did not want an interruption. I had no idea what to do until I saw Treasury Secretary John Connally. When I explained to him why he would have to wait before going in for the prayer breakfast, he entered the room, gently explained the situation to Erlichman, and my problem was solved!

The White House staff prayer group continued to grow. One day, a year after I had left the White House, a friend of mine called from Washington. The telephone almost pulsed with his excitement. "Guess who the speakers were this morning at the White House breakfast," he shouted. "Who?" I asked, thinking there was no possible way he could surprise me.

But surprise me he did. "Chuck Colson and Harold Hughes—together!" he said.

That was the first I had heard of the conversion of Colson. All I could think about was the tough, arrogant politician I had known whom I did not even include on my prayer breakfast invitation list. And Harold Hughes—that was as big a surprise as I could get. I had met Hughes through the Fellowship Foundation and had even corresponded with him. In fact, I used to wonder what someone like Colson would do if he knew I was writing Hughes. For he was a Democrat, the political "enemy" to the White House of those days. And now here was my friend, telling me that not only was Hughes at the White House, but he was there as Colson's guest!

Nixon himself never attended the staff prayer breakfasts. I never really knew whether he was even aware of them. But Gerald Ford did attend whenever he could.

It was at one of the prayer breakfasts at the White House that I first met Doug Coe. As my friendship with him deepened after that first meeting, I became aware that my spiritual pulse was beating in a way it had not in a long time. Coe had no idea I was an ordained minister. He targeted me for one of the people he would "disciple." During that period of my life, I had grown cold on spiritual matters. My involvement with the prayer group was a way of reaching out and trying to find again the joy I had once known in Christ. And because of the work of Doug Coe and others within our fellowship, I opened my life to God again. Within nine months after leaving the White House, I was back in the church-related ministry, after nearly a decade's absence. (See my book, *The White House Mystique,* for that story.)

It was also through Coe that I learned our White House group was just one among a multitude of cells meeting all over Washington for prayer and Bible study.

As much as one-third of the Senate, for example, has been involved in prayer and sharing groups at one time. In fact, the Senate and House groups may be the best instruments in Washington for overcoming partisan division. In the Senate group, James Allen, Alabama's conservative, might be praying with Mark Hatfield, a Republican from Oregon with liberal leanings. This basis for meeting is far different from hacking out compromises on legislation, or debating issues.

In 1969, Senator Hatfield wrote President Nixon about the prayer groups. "In my experience," said the Senator, "this type of relationship has brought about an ability to discuss hard issues in a spirit of reconciliation as well as the opportunity to be frank and honest and still disagree. Perhaps the biggest factor is the confidence and trust that is built up between men who normally have every reason to distrust one another."

The seeds which would grow into the Senate prayer group apparently were sown in 1941, when journalist David Lawrence and three senators met to pray the day after Pearl Harbor. With encouragement from Abram Vereide, the meetings continued. The format for the sessions now is much like it is at the White House—prayer, a devotional, and discussion around the table.

There is a similar style in the House of Representatives, whose prayer meetings were launched around 1943. Congressman Walter Judd of Minnesota—and a former missionary to China—met with some of his colleagues for prayer on Thursday mornings. They included Brooks Hays of Arkansas who would later become a president of the Southern

Baptist Convention. Also in the group was Arizona's John Murdock, Paul Cunningham of Iowa and others. It was Vereide who suggested that the House group begin meeting for breakfast.

"Because of the prayer breakfasts, Thursday is the best day of the week for me," said Mississippi Congressman G. V. "Sonny" Montgomery. "I have a great feeling of personal renewal, because I have been provided an opportunity to experience religious fellowship with my colleagues."

One congressman remarked that the prayer breakfast is the only meeting in Washington for which he does not mind arriving 15 minutes early and staying late.

Those who participate in the many prayer groups find, on leaving Washington, that they have grown accustomed to an experience they do not want to lose. The result is that the Washington ministries have helped spark other groups and cells wherever the Washington folk move.

Take, for example, Cal Thomas. Once, while I was still in the White House, I was invited to speak for one of the Washington cells. A tall, mustachioed fellow identified himself as Cal Thomas, a newsman with NBC. Later in the week, Cal invited me out to lunch with him. I discovered that he and his wife, Rae, were active in the prayer group ministries and had been for some time.

Sometime later, Cal and Rae moved to Houston, where Cal became a commentator with a local station. But his home became a center for Bible study and sharing groups. Often Rae would rise early and cook breakfast for the folk as they came for Bible study and prayer.

Groups like those which influenced Cal and Rae are sprinkled throughout Washington. A walk through a composite Washington day illustrates the scope of the prayer groups meeting in the city.

The day begins with a breakfast in a dining room in the United States Capitol. Fred Heyn of the Fellowship Foundation shares the meal with a group of American Indians who work in the government and other institutions. Downtown near the White House, a group of judges and lawyers are beginning their prayer period.

At the noon hour, several downtown workers sit down for lunch at New York Avenue Presbyterian Church. Fred Rhodes, a former deputy director of the Veterans Administration, is the leader on this particular day. Rhodes is also a former vice president of the Southern Baptist Convention.

A large group is assembling at the Pentagon. Two prayer cells are convening at the State Department. A few workers at the Department of Agriculture are slipping into the auditorium of the main building off 14th Street.

It would be wrong to assume that these prayer cells involve the majority of Washington's workers. Nor is every participant a vibrant, witnessing Christian. But hundreds of lives are being affected daily.

One prayer group participant put it like this:

> Sometimes working in Washington is like being in a hurricane. The pressures and winds crush

76

and blow. You reach out for something solid to cling to. A lot of Washingtonians grasp at cocktail party relationships, or political alliances. But all these are passing. Getting with the prayer cell anchors me to Christ.

CHAPTER VII

Religion on Embassy Row

For a man thought by some to be plotting the takeover of America, Bill Bright is surprisingly gentle, bordering on meekness. Yet, the Christian Embassy—an idea of Bright's—is apparently thought by some Washington observers to be the center of an evangelical/right-wing plot to take over America.

Sojourners magazine titled its piece on the embassy and what it felt to be related matters in headlines slightly reminiscent of the period of yellow journalism:

The Plan To Save America:
A Disclosure of an Alarming Political Initiative by the Evangelical Far Right

Of all the mainline evangelical efforts to minister in Washington, none has caught the ire of national media quite to the extent Campus Crusade and the

Christian Embassy have. *Newsweek* magazine gave a page and a third of its September 6, 1976, issue for what was largely a condensation of the *Sojourners* article (see next chapter).

Even Billy Graham was drawn into the fracas. He reported he had been told Bright was trying to organize groups growing out of the Graham crusades into political units. Bright quickly responded, in a conversation with Graham, that it was not so. Later Graham backed away and indicated there was not the split between him and Bright that some observers had concluded was opening up.

What is it about Campus Crusade and the Christian Embassy which draws such fire? Probably the central cause is that Campus Crusade and the Embassy are so open about their objectives and so aggressive about carrying them out.

"The Christian Embassy is designed to communicate the claims of Christ to official Washington and the diplomatic community," says Swede Anderson, its director. And as we will see momentarily, the methodology is much the same as Campus Crusade has used effectively on college campuses and elsewhere.

Perhaps another reason for the ire drawn by the Embassy's ministry is an apparent identification with strengthening the nation by winning it to Christ. *Sojourners* quoted, in the April, 1976, issue, Rolfe McCollister, a Louisiana businessman and friend of Bright. McCollister serves as president of the Christian Embassy. *Sojourners* quoted him:

We stand for a strong America. We want

America to be a Christian country. We began as a
Christian nation, but we no longer are. We want
a more Christian government. We plan to do that
by evangelizing official Washington, by working
with men in the executive branch, the Congress,
the judiciary, the military and the diplomatic service, and by ministering to their families in an
effort to change non-Christian official Washington to Christian official Washington.

To some that smacks of cultural religion, and there-
in lies some of their objection to the Christian Embassy's approach.

But Bright does not see it that way. His purposes
are designed primarily to introduce people to a relationship with God through Christ. If a stronger nation is a result, it is a secondary one, an extra benefit
thrown in.

Bright has also been attacked for a pamphlet he
wrote, entitled, "Your Five Duties as a Christian
Citizen." Some again saw signs of an ominous plot
by a group of Christians to take over the nation. But
Bright supported no political line in the pamphlet;
he just cannot conceive of the Christian life being
lived in isolation from the political process. The ac-
cusation is that Bright is too far to the right politically, too conservative. But if that were the case, he
would not have written a document urging higher
voter registration. For the conventional political
wisdom in America is that higher registrations tend
to benefit the Democrats, who constitute the more
leftward of the country's two major parties.

The Christian Embassy opened in 1975. Some
time before, in an executive seminar, Bright had

shared his vision for such a ministry in Washington. McCollister was infected with the idea, and told Bright he thought it was a "tremendous idea." Later he telephoned Bright and reiterated that he was still "really serious" about helping launch the project.

A core group of men were assembled to sit on the Embassy's board. It was decided it would have no legal union with Campus Crusade but be a separate entity.

A search was made for a facility for the Christian Embassy. The building found was the Chase mansion which at the time was owned by the Roman Catholic Archdiocese of Washington. The $1,000,000 needed for purchasing and refurbishing the large house was raised through businessmen.

The board asked Campus Crusade to provide staff for the Embassy. Bright and McCollister were both convinced Anderson was the man for the directorship of the project. Anderson had been working with Campus Crusade since his student days at the University of Colorado. Part of his service for the organization had been in Latin America. He and McCollister had met in travels on Campus Crusade business.

In addition to Anderson, 17 other Campus Crusade staff members were brought in to work in the Embassy.

Would there be tension—even a spirit of competitiveness—between the Christian Embassy and similar ministries, like Fellowship House? Anderson responds, "We have great mutual respect and love for one another. I'm concerned that people see us as loving one another and expressing the unity of the Body of Christ.''

Basic to Campus Crusade's aims is to help new and long-time Christians mature in their witnessing. "There are three aspects of making disciples," says a Campus Crusade training manual (for the Intermediate Discipleship Training Class). The three aspects are evangelism, follow-up and discipling.

The same philosophy underlies methods used through the Christian Embassy.

The evangelism phase will take many forms. Swede Anderson himself will make personal visits to officials, whenever possible. There are events at the Embassy which provide the setting for sharing.

For example, a Christian official and his wife may host a small group of their peers for dinner in the elegant surroundings. The conversation will be steered to Christ, and the Christians will quietly share their own experience with God.

When individuals make a commitment to Christ, the follow-up and discipling phases begin. Often these are through group Bible studies and discipleship classes. There are such study groups now in the United States Capitol. Though Anderson will not disclose names of people being reached, they include congressional aides as well as their principals.

Aside from thrusting the Gospel into the official institutions of Washington, the Christian Embassy seeks to penetrate another vital Washington institution—the home. This part of the work is often carried by the Embassy's women staffers.

They conduct neighborhood Bible studies. Sometimes the groups meet in the homes of congressional wives. And those congressional wives will sponsor occasional buffet dinners at the Christian Embassy, bringing their husbands along.

The Christian Embassy also seeks to minister to children of official Washington. Often Embassy staff will help refer newcomers' teens and younger children to other Christian groups, such as the Navigators. And the Embassy will conduct activities for the children, such as a picnic and sports-oriented party, complete with famed athletes as guests.

The earliest discussions between Bright and McCollister regarding the Christian Embassy idea took place on a trip they made together to Latin America. Several times they were reminded that they should have met with the Washington embassies of the countries they were visiting. They began thinking of the foreign embassies in Washington and their needs. The idea expanded considerably from that, but the Embassy still hopes to reach out to Washington's diplomatic community.

One way relationships are established with the diplomats is by inviting them in to the Christian Embassy. Here they discuss their countries with Christian groups planning trips abroad.

For example, a group was going to visit South Africa. Members of that country's Washington Embassy attended a dinner party at the Christian Embassy. After dinner and discussion of South Africa, the Christians shared with the diplomats the mes-

sage of Christ in what McCollister calls "a very limited way."

A composite day in the life of the Christian Embassy might look like this:

The day begins with several groups of the city's
officialdom gathering for Embassy-related ministries. One group assembles for breakfast, prayer and
Bible study at the Embassy with Dr. Bill Bright,
who happens to be in town. Swede Anderson is at
the Capitol, meeting with another early morning
group.

As the day progresses, more encounters take
place. At the lunch hour several congressional aides
come together for more Bible study. Women staff
from the Christian Embassy convene with secre-
tarial staffs of government offices.

Late afternoon will see a concentration on personal visits by Embassy personnel to offices
throughout official Washington.

In the evening the Embassy will host small dinners, where Christ ultimately becomes the topic of
conversation.

But are the officials contacted during this day
really open to these evangelistic efforts? Or are they
simply practicing some diplomacy themselves?

"We find official Washington very open," says
McCollister. "It is assumed that such people are
inaccessible, but they are not. All have needs; they
are lonely, too, and are pleased when we contact
them."

McCollister hopes other Christian groups will
begin to use the Embassy. This is one of the reasons

for establishing a broad-based advisory board, consisting of people like Billy Graham, Norman Vincent Peale and W. A. Criswell. The idea is that such men would have a headquarters for ministry during trips to Washington. In fact, the only accommodations at the Embassy—except for a live-in housekeeping couple—are for such Christian leaders who may be involved in Embassy-related activities while in Washington.

McCollister also stresses the fact that there is no relationship between the Christian Embassy and such groups as the Freedom Foundation, or Third Century Publishers, as implied by *Sojourners*.

"We accept Washington the way we find it," says McCollister. "Our concern is that when politicians come here, we are there to help."

McCollister continues: "We would hope to serve the needs of officials who are not Christians, and of course we would hope they would become Christians. Our task is not to get Christians elected to office. We simply want to be there to minister to Christians and non-Christians alike."

CHAPTER VIII

Missionaries to the Unmighty

The member of the Washington housing board blinked as he went out his front door on his way to work. There in front of his house were two large cardboard shanty-houses. Inside were several folk who themselves were just beginning to stir after a night spent in the cardboard structures.

That is a possible scenario for the Sojourners, a Christian ministry community whose idea of missions in Washington is a pole away from most of the other evangelical organizations. In fact, the Sojourners might be called "missionaries to the unmighty."

Far from the gray-granite and splendidly dressed houses of Northwest Washington and Embassy Row is another city. The geographical distance may not be more than a few miles. But the social, economic and philosophical differences are light years in span. The other city is a labyrinth of yawning hulks, boarded up since the riots of 1967, in many cases. Stretches of the city look like Dresden after World War II. The tragic irony is that many of the houses shuttered with rotting timber could be made habitable for many in Washington who are homeless. The regiments of row houses help constitute the Washington ghettos—some of which stare at the dome of the United States Capitol gleaming like a cotton-candy ball over the city.

Life in the Washington ghetto is little different from what it is in economically depressed areas of Chicago, Detroit, or New York. In 1975, gun homicides among urban ghetto dwellers were 10 times what they were in the rest of the nation. The crime rate in Washington is legendary. A major reason is the despair and hopelessness with which the city's impoverished areas are impregnated.

I was driving an out-of-town visitor through the District of Columbia one night. The brilliant orange street lamps bathed the White House in daylight-looking brightness. But even those lamps were a concession to the terror night can sometimes be in the capital of the United States. And my friend turned and exclaimed: "I don't see anybody getting mugged!" Such is the legend of crime in the city. People expect to see it as much as they do big black cars.

While others are aiming ministry at leadership levels, the Sojourners work in that cosmos of calamity, violent crime and helplessness.

The most visible aspect of the Sojourners' work nationally is their magazine. In 1975 they changed the name of their magazine, the *Post-American,* and began a new thrust under the title *Sojourners*. The objective of the magazine now is spelled out on its cover: **Discerning the times through the life and faith of biblical people.**

"The magazine exists to be a voice helping to rebuild the church to what God wants it to be," says Joe Roos, a native of Kansas City, Missouri, who is on the publication's staff. "The church in America," he continues, "is too often conformed to the nation's social and cultural values. A basic rebuilding step for the church is to begin to live under the values of the Kingdom of God."

Paul's admonition of non-conformity in Romans 12:2 is a pivotal text for the Sojourners. There, Paul wrote this: "And be not conformed to this world: but be ye transformed by the renewing of your mind, that ye may prove what is that good, and acceptable, and perfect, will of God."

Even in routine matters of daily living, the Sojourners try to strike the non-conformist style. The magazine staff itself, for example, comes from a group of some 40 to 50 people who live together in what Roos calls a "Christian community." Their desire is to live in Washington's most impoverished areas to be near the poor.

"The main thing we had in mind," says Roos, "was to live in the context of the poor urban environment where we could live out the scriptural imperative to identify with the poor." Actually living with the poor is the central focus of the Sojourners community, not just social action, he explains.

In the early days of its existence, the group was

"more prophetic," more strictly a social-action body. Now, it sees itself more as "church," the Body of Christ. The conversion came, says Roos, as the community acquired a "real strong pastoral sense, the healing of ourselves and those around us." That outward-moving "healing" generated a focus on social injustice within Washington.

"Our main purpose of identity is to live with the poor and be the Body of Christ in that context. We're not trying to influence directly what's going on in Washington. Just being the church is the most political act you can do in Washington!" says Roos.

Newsweek magazine called the *Sojourners* periodical "a Washington monthly of radical Christian opinion" *(Newsweek,* September 6, 1976, p. 51). As far as the Sojourners are concerned, the "radical" tag has more to do with Reformation theology than with mere politics. They find heavy identity with such historic groups as the Anabaptists. A look at the Anabaptists provides insight into what sparks the Sojourners.

The Protestant Reformation of the 16th century was launched by the German monk, Martin Luther, in 1517. As the Reformation developed, three prongs emerged. Two of them—the Lutheran and Reformed (under Zwingli)—took rather prosaic patterns. They organized into institutional churches, which ultimately became state churches.

But the third prong took a definitely radical twist. The Anabaptists desired most of all to create voluntary societies of Christians. The Sermon on the Mount would be central to their belief and practice.

The pastoral sense of caring for one another's needs would be strong in the community. And they would insist that the church be free of any cultural hold by its society. In *The Growth of the Christian Church,* Robert Hastings Nichols described the Anabaptist view like this: "A church under the power of civil rulers who may or may not be Christians, they held, is no true church. Thus they separated themselves from fellowship with the churches of the Reformation, all of which were state churches" (p. 230). The Anabaptists came under intense persecution from both the Protestant state churches and from Roman Catholics, especially in the Netherlands.

Their cousins in Washington—the Sojourners—do not bar themselves from cooperation and interaction with other churches, however. And within the Sojourners community, there is a wide variety of denominational background. They even find agreement with aspects of Catholicism, especially the stress they feel Catholic theology makes on the church as the Body of Christ.

"A lot of us have evangelical Christian backgrounds," says Roos. "But our view of salvation distinguishes us from other groups," he says. The Sojourners do not believe the emphasis is as much on individual witness as on that of the Body. "We feel more about giving God's saving Presence in terms of God working through His people. It is the Body that God works through; this is much broader than just personal salvation," says Roos.

This is the base for the Sojourners' ministries in Washington. For the neighborhood where the community resides, its work is of the most basic type. The Sojourners operate a tutoring program. They are at work in establishing a food cooperative. There is even a "soup line."

Housing is also a central focus of the ministry of the Sojourners. They see a glaring contradiction in the fact that people—poor people—are being evicted from their homes, while so many row houses stand empty. But simply lobbying for a change in housing policies is not for the Sojourners. "Our experience convinces us we must do more than that," says Roos. That is where the cardboard shanty-houses come in. "By our actions we hope to demonstrate what the plight of the poor really is," Roos says. Thus, the group maps out a program of non-violent public action.

The Sojourners community has not won, and likely will not win, supporters in the deeply conservative evangelical community. The magazine's greatest national exposure came when it published several articles alleging links between Bill Bright of Campus Crusade and a plan *Sojourners* said the "evangelical far right" had to save the country.

In the magazine piece, *Sojourners* suggested there was a tie between Third Century Publishers, a politically conservative organization; the Christian Embassy, which is related to Campus Crusade; and "Here's Life America," another Crusade program. The magazine implied that these were tools to politicize the evangelical right wing, even to the point of taking over local political precincts.

Bill Bright denies suggestions that there is any

partisanship to his efforts to waken Americans to responsible citizenship. "Not even my wife knows how I voted in 1976," says Bright.

The *Sojourners* article made the following allegations:

> Events and activities in the last twenty months point to a major initiative by the evangelical far right in this country. New organizations have been created, an older right wing group revitalized, and the top leadership of a huge evangelistic organization has become involved in plans with a clear political purpose [from the April, 1976, issue].

Bright contends, however, that his desire is to encourage Christians to apply their values to their political responsibilities, whether such application produces liberal or conservative responses. That is a goal similar to the Sojourners.

Whatever the outcome, the article was illustrative of the aim of the magazine—to call the American church and religious community to a stance apart from their culture. And whatever impact the Sojourners have on leadership levels in Washington is indirect. But if Christians in such positions are motivated to apply the values of God's Kingdom to what they are doing in their positions of power, Sojourners will have felt it has fulfilled its purpose.

CHAPTER IX

The President's Pastor

When Dr. Charles Trentham became pastor of Washington's First Baptist Church in 1974, a Georgian named Jimmy Carter was beginning a long struggle to introduce himself to America. For Dr. Trentham, it seemed he was faced with an almost impossible task of restoring vitality to an aging inner city church whose life had nearly been snuffed out by the urban violence in Washington in the late sixties. Most early observers passed off Jimmy Carter's wanderings across America as voyages into the seas of futility.

Observers of both Jimmy Carter and Charles Trentham were in for a surprise. Jimmy Carter was elected President. Charles Trentham became his pastor and found that what he thought would be a pulpit of at least some limited importance suddenly became one to which the ears of the world were turned.

Carter announced during his campaign that, if

elected, he would join the Baptist church nearest the White House. Baptists are not a credal denomination, but many of them take seriously what they call the "Church Covenant." There, it states: "We ... engage that when we remove from this place we will, as soon as possible, unite with some other church where we can carry out the spirit of this covenant and the principles of God's Word." For many years, the interpretation of that phrase was that a Baptist would relocate to the church nearest his new residence. The age of mobility changed the words but not the attitude in Baptists who had heard the Covenant all their days.

First Baptist Church of Washington, at 1328 16th Street, Northwest, is close to the White House.

Since the late sixties, First Baptist Church had been in a state of decline. Increasing urban crime had pushed Washingtonians to the suburbs. Not only was the church losing people, but its budgets were running in the red.

In recent months things have turned around. They had begun reversing before Carter came to town. The church closed out its finances for 1976 in the black.

Publicity about Carter's possible move to First Baptist helped some. But people are also moving back into the District of Columbia. "There's an upsurge in church attendance across the land," says Pastor Trentham. "The Gallup Poll shows an increase in adult church attendance," notes Trentham, who feels his church is also benefiting from that general trend.

In 1974 Trentham understood he was facing a unique challenge. "I saw First Baptist as having a national pulpit then," he says. A third of the people attending worship services in those days were visitors. Since First Baptist is also close to Embassy Row, many were from foreign embassies.

Like most inner city Washington churches, First Baptist is multi-racial. The participants from the embassies accent the color varieties at First Baptist.

Representatives of the embassies of such countries as the Cameroon and Liberia will occasionally attend. President Tolbert of Liberia has worshipped there when in Washington. There will also be other racial groups, as diverse as Chinese and Germans, in the congregation.

Rosalynn Carter was especially interested in the work of First Baptist Church with mental patients. For some time, the congregation has worked with outpatients of St. Elizabeth Hospital in this ministry. Mrs. Carter had been concerned with mental health projects while her husband was governor of Georgia.

Associate Pastor Chuck Sanks works with the chaplain at St. Elizabeth's and members of the First Baptist congregation in the program. Regularly the patients meet at the church for a meal, handcraft instruction, games. "It's a meeting place for people who are lonely and overlooked," says Trentham.

"Bread for the City" is another facet of First Baptist's outreach. In this program, the church is in partnership with other downtown Washington congregations—Foundry United Methodist, Luther

Place Lutheran, National City Christian and St. Matthew Catholic Church.

The work of "Bread for the City" is to help feed people "who are not destitute, but find that their money is buying less in Washington's constantly increasing cost-of-living situation," Trentham explains. Such people are embarrassed to go to welfare agencies, and so they can come to the churches.

In addition to food, "Bread for the City" helps with medical services, clothing and a range of other services.

Many of those helped are retired government workers. They had lived in downtown Washington when it was the main residential area for federal employees in the thirties and forties. When the rush out to the suburbs began, they would not or could not move, because of limited pensions. But they were also squeezed by the higher prices of Washington itself. They really could not live *anywhere*— many of them had no relatives elsewhere, since they were elderly. "Bread for the City" was created for their special needs.

So the mix of people with whom Jimmy Carter worships is wide. Racially, culturally, economically, the church is a microcosm of the world which is Carter's daily concern.

When Charles Trentham first became aware that Jimmy Carter would likely be part of First Baptist Church, Trentham told him, "We would try to be a church that would never be in your way when we're not needed, but would never be out of your way when we are needed."

Carter had indicated an interest in teaching Sunday School, something he had been doing at the Plains, Georgia, Baptist Church for a long time. But every church knows how important it is that its teachers be regular in attendance. Could a man who was "on call" to a nation 24 hours a day mesh into a church Bible-teaching program?

There was no problem at First Baptist. Most of the church's teaching programs are set up on a quarterly basis. Sometimes a teacher will be responsible only for a month, or even as little as one week at a time.

Trentham himself is a teaching pastor. His scholarly approach is almost professorial, without sacrificing warmth and compassion. His preaching is Bible-centered—he has authored commentaries on Bible books. He has been a seminary professor as well as Dean of the School of Religion at the University of Tennessee in Knoxville.

He served that city's First Baptist Church for 21 years prior to going to Washington. For 12 of those years he simultaneously held the University of Tennessee post. All of that, Trentham now feels, was preparation for the work he is now doing.

Being the President's pastor stamps Trentham with immense prestige. But his concerns remain the basic ones he had when he first came to Washington in 1974.

"I want to help meet the needs of people locked in boredom," he says now. "So many of them are on a treadmill, just waiting to go home from here. Others are climbing the ladder of success. It all calls for a special ministry of teaching the sustaining grace of God even while on the treadmill, and guidance for those wanting to achieve from humanitarian standpoints."

And Washington casts an extra dimension in the preaching and teaching interests of the President's pastor. "The responsible use of power is an area the church has often overlooked in its teaching," believes Trentham. "What we can do in public for the underprivileged is much more than we can do on the private level."

The multitudes of press people who trail the President to church insure that Trentham's preaching is not only on the private level. The presence of the man from Plains guarantees that the man from Knoxville will be one of the most public preachers in America. Anyone who knows Charles Trentham believes that is exactly as God arranged it.

CHAPTER X

Capital Churches

COLUMBIA BAPTIST CHURCH

The family was a little nervous as it walked the aisle to unite with Columbia Baptist Church. For nine months they had probed Washington for just the right congregation. They had come from a Baptist church in the deep south. The fellowship had been rich in their churches back home. But soon after moving to the Washington area, cultural shock had benumbed them. They had little hope of finding the warmth they had been accustomed to.

But at the conclusion of the worship service, Columbia's pastor, Neal Jones, was seeing to it the family was ushered to a section of the church where they could meet everyone. Then, as if Pastor Jones sensed the special need of the family, he was steering them into a dining room. There they would have Sunday lunch with a small group of Columbia members and other newcomers. By that afternoon, the family was feeling the close personal relationships it had searched for over the nine months.

Columbia Baptist Church is located in Falls Church, Virginia, just two miles from the District of Columbia line. Its stately colonial buildings house sets of ministries designed to reach the deepest needs of the Washington community.

"The urban loneliness here can be tragic," says Jones in his soft Texas drawl. "The best ministry is to help people relate to a community of other people—the church." The impact, he says, is especially hard on the family of the Washington worker. "The breadwinner is caught up in the world of his work. If the family is not helped, the results are tragic," continues Jones.

"One of the things that worries me in Washington is that the para-church groups have the inroads to the top men. But what about their families? Who ministers to them? Where is the church in all this?"

There is little question about where Columbia Baptist Chruch is. Its stress on the family nature of the church community begins in its worship style. Sunday mornings emphasize the theme of the Fatherhood of God. Informal Sunday night services focus on the family of God.

While a traditional worship approach holds sway at Columbia's two morning worship services, innovation is the norm for Sunday nights. Often Jones will turn the evening service into a Christian version of a talk-show. He will interview guests, letting them share what it means to practice the Christian faith in their daily setting. Sometimes the guests will be non-members of Columbia—occasionally, celebrities. But most often, Jones' partners in conversation are Columbia members.

The worship-style lays a theological foundation on which a broad diversity of weekday ministries is built. Realizing that Washington's high living costs demand that both parents work in many cases, the church has established a comprehensive day-care program. Some 200 children are cared for daily through this ministry.

Dr. Dale Keeton, a Christian psychologist, is on Columbia's staff. He maintains a full personal counseling program, on an appointment basis. Additionally, Dr. Keeton provides group studies in Parent Effectiveness Training, couples' communications and a number of other areas.

Washington has a massive international community. Columbia has sought to minister to this group through English classes. In fact, Columbia members spent a total of 1,064 hours teaching English as a second language during one year.

Near Front Royal in northern Virginia, Columbia owns a retreat center. Recently, it has been involved in construction of a $250,000 building at the center. The objective of the facility is to help deepen lasting relationships among the people. "On Sunday we just get a taste of fellowship," says Jones. "When you spend 24-48 hours together, you begin to develop close relationships. God is just not going to let people get right with Him until they get right with one another. God never said we could make it alone—we did."

Newcomers to Washington find that ministries like those at Columbia go a long way in squelching that sense of being isolated in the middle of a crowd.

FOURTH PRESBYTERIAN CHURCH

Richard Halverson, minister of Washington's Fourth Presbyterian Church, looks as sage as Solomon. And many Washingtonians have discovered that Dick Halverson's knowledge is broad. His many gifts have enabled him to make an indelible stamp on the lives of thousands—ranging from reputed Watergate burglar James McCord, to former Senator Harold Hughes.

Once I was present in a tension-sparked room in Latin America. A noted politician had just made a statement that could have set off a fire of argument. No one could think of just how to respond. Then Halverson began to speak quiet, healing words. And I thought: Kissinger should have his diplomatic finesse!

But it was much more than diplomatic finesse. Halverson has a keen grasp of how to relate the Bible to historical circumstances. Halverson relates better to people in power than any minister I know in Washington. He is the chaplain of sorts to the Fellowship Foundation. Often Halverson and Doug Coe will spend hours counseling together on the theological aspects of their work.

Halverson came to Washington from California, where he had been on the staff of Hollywood's First Presbyterian Church. Early in his life he had experience with jobs outside the church. The background has left him with an understanding of the laymen to whom he ministers.

Hundreds of people in positions of power outside Washington are touched by Halverson's ministry through a newsletter he edits, entitled *Perspective.* Through this newsletter he relates the Christian faith to matters of everyday business and living in general. Sometimes the newsletter will discuss precepts and dimensions of Christ's teaching that often go unemphasized. Always the letters are brief. And the sentences are written in Halverson's staccato, to-the-point style. The objective of *Perspective* is exactly what the title implies—to give its readers a different way of looking at their responsibilities and opportunities.

As with Columbia Baptist, Fourth Presbyterian's Sunday worship style belies its total approach to ministry. Though hundreds may be present at the three worship services, the atmosphere is that of intimate small-group worship. During the worship service those present might be asked to link hands and sing, or greet one another individually.

Though Fourth Presbyterian is a large church, the small-group method is utilized through the week. It is through such person-to-person ministries that Fourth extends its ministry into the wider Washington community. Such groups will center themselves on weekday Bible study and prayer periods. Members will seek out individual opportunities to serve, such as in personal counseling.

Overall, most everything Fourth Presbyterian

does is aimed at helping Christians come into contact with individuals with particular needs, as Jesus Christ did, on a one-to-one basis.

CAPITOL HILL METROPOLITAN BAPTIST CHURCH

What do you do when you are a native of the Middle East who suddenly finds yourself living within blocks of the United States Capitol? You are a Coptic Christian. Questions dart through your head: Where can you find fellowship with other Christians? Even if you find a Christian community nearby, can you be sure they will accept you?

Those were the precise circumstances of one young man who arrived recently in Washington. And he did find a Christian group who would fellowship with him happily. They were part of the Capitol Hill Metropolitan Baptist Church.

The designation "Capitol Hill" is exactly right. The church is located five blocks from the Library of Congress and six blocks from the United States Capitol building.

The church feels a special responsibility for the hundreds of staff aides who work in the labyrinth of the Capitol and other institutions in the Hill complex. "These are the people who are here and most often neglected," says Wade Freeman, pastor of the Capitol Hill church.

In 1976 Americans became more acutely aware of the Hill aide, as newspaper stories disclosed misbehavior in some important offices at the Capitol.

More and more of the aides—and their bosses—are moving back to Capitol Hill after several years' absence from the area as a residential section.

For many years, however, Capitol Hill church has maintained housing for young singles. Two dormitory-type facilities on East Capitol Street are open for men and women, many of whom work in government offices on the Hill and elsewhere.

There is a social program and Bible teaching ministry for the working singles, led by Associate Pastor Dick Logsdon. The church is interested in touching the people whether they are members of the church or not. In fact, only about half of the participants are members of the Capitol Hill church.

Because of its unique location, the church has been selected by agencies of the Southern Baptist Convention as a laboratory for studying and teaching urban ministry.

The Capitol Hill church is markedly different from other inner-city churches, because it is about to see its community undergo a second transitional stage.

The first occurred when the area just around the Capitol—and the church—changed in the late fifties and sixties. Affluent people who had lived in the row houses began moving to Georgetown, or the Virginia and Maryland suburbs. The community rapidly became poor and crime-ridden.

But the pattern had been reversed by the mid-seventies. The neighborhood was becoming fashionable again. Now people were moving out of Georgetown back to the Hill. Dilapidated houses were being renovated. Their prices were soaring.

Capitol Hill Metropolitan Baptist Church had sought to minister to the community when it was poor. Now it was facing an entirely different set of needs—those of young marrieds and singles on the way up. Sometimes they were harder to reach than their predecessors.

As Pastor Freeman talked one chilly January day, a group of retired people had gathered in the church fellowship hall. "These are some of the people who came in when the cost of the houses was low," he said. "I'm afraid they're not going to be able to stay much longer because of the property tax increases. People on fixed pensions just can't hack these costs."

Replacing some of those who will leave are about 70 members of Congress. Freeman hopes they will find the kind of welcome at the Capitol Hill church that one western congressman did. Upon Jimmy Carter's election, the House member wrote the President-elect that he should consider attending the Capitol Hill Metropolitan Baptist Church. "I happened on the ... church two years ago," the congressman wrote the President-elect. "I found I liked it, and I'm sure you would."

Southern Baptists hope the church will be able to intensify its ministries, not only to official Washington, but to the city as a whole. The Home Mission Board of the Southern Baptist Convention has spent nearly $50,000 to place urban-ministry interns at its training center in the Capitol Hill church.

Academic work is under the supervision of

Southeastern Baptist Theological Seminary in Wake
Forest, North Carolina. The seminary now considers the church an extension of itself. Interns working in the program will get credit toward doctoral
degrees.

The program was designed for the District of Columbia, though it is hoped it will be a model for other
inner city ministries. Participants from New York
and Baltimore are involved. Among other things,
they are studying how churches survive and meet
the needs of changing neighborhoods, as well as
community ministries.

THE CHURCH OF THE SAVIOR

The Church of the Savior has more than 100
ministers seeking to probe and meet the needs of
Washington. Actually, not all 100 are on the paid
staff of the church. But every member of Church of
the Savior is ordained to the ministry.

Ask John Owens what his work is, and he probably will not tell you first that he is a clinical psychologist. He will likely respond by describing the kind
of ministry in which he is involved.

And for Owens, that ministry is through
Dunamis Vocations, a "sister community" of this
church. Actually the Church of the Savior is no
longer "the Church." Under a recent restructuring,
members of the Church of the Savior have grouped
themselves into smaller units described as sister
communities, and each is now a church. The
Dunamis Vocations Church has a primary commit-

ment to the *Dunamis* mission in which 30 to 35 people are involved in Washington.

Dunamis is a mission, originating within the Church of the Savior, to official Washington. Its basic objective is to enable its members to develop personal relationships with congressmen, so that they (the church members) can perform a pastoral-prophetic role.

"It is never our intent to be a lobbying or influence group," says Owens. "We're concerned about being a caring community in relationship to individual persons."

But issues before Congress and the nation are at the center of focus for the *Dunamis* teams. "We exist to be on the side of the poor and oppressed," says Marion Franz, staff person for *Dunamis*. "We form groups around issues toward which we are called, then work with congressional committees established on those issues."

She continues: "We realize the church is called to speak the Word. Our prophetic role is whatever flows from that. It is not an attempt to switch votes on issues. Whatever we do on the prophetic level is in a pastoral sense." Praying for people in power and the issues with which they work is a major activity of the *Dunamis* workers.

Dunamis groups are now formed around such concerns as prison reform, the problems of American Indians, military spending, education. The people in each group become acquainted with the congressional committee with jurisdiction over their interest area. Each member will select a congressman who sits on the committee in question. They will seek to develop a personal relationship with him, and they will make a regular commitment to pray for him.

"The objective is to develop the personal, pastor-prophet relationship; if after that there's opportunity to express an opinion, then it's there," says Owens.

The Church of the Savior is noted for the disciplines it asks its members to adopt. Among those disciplines is a commitment to tithe income and spend at least 45 minuets every day in prayer, Bible study and journal work. Additionally, each member must link with a task force—like the *Dunamis* groups.

"One's personal growth is basic," says Owens. "It is a discipline of becoming a person capable of seeing visions of newness, or things not good, and to see such things with the clarity of being able to relate and interpret these visions," he adds.

As to method, the *Dunamis* groups use a wide variety of tools. Sometimes members of Congress are invited to meet with a *Dunamis* group. And there are periodic institutes on critical issues, sponsored by *Dunamis* groups. Weekly, the *Dunamis* Vocations Churches meet for Bible discussion, prayer, update on their issues and a period for members to give an account of how they personally are relating to the disciplines.

Often the groups will meet in a room they have on Capitol Hill. The room is also used for Bible studies by other groups—such as by members of the staff of the National Governors Conference.

Dunamis' primary concern is not to address the issues of state faced by the congress members but to allow the Holy Spirit to minister to the personal needs of the members of Congress. This comes as the personal relationships are deepened.

The word *Dunamis* is the Greek word the New Testament uses in talking about the *power* of the Holy Spirit. *Dunamis* members do not use position to achieve their aims. They seem to take seriously Jesus' statement that the meek will inherit the earth. Consequently, they work on the premise that the power of the Holy Spirit is as much in twentieth century Washington as it was in post-resurrection Jerusalem.

CHAPTER XI

Has It Made Any Difference?

There they were again. The ivory buildings of Washington once more were slipping under my airplane. It had been a long time since those first flights into the city. Then, I had been an awed newcomer, and the structures had a golden tint in the afternoon sun of those days. Now I was coming to Washington again, but not to be met by a limousine, not as part of the Washington community. This time I came as a watcher. My host was unnumbered. And in the dull gray morning, the buildings appeared not as washed ivory or baskets of gold but as dirty rocks.

My feeling was different now. In the early days when I would look at the city, I would wonder if anybody cared for the bureaucrat. After having lived there and after having been plunged into the caldron of feverish activity, I knew. There were many who cared.

I gazed across the Mall to the Capitol. No longer was it a defying fortress peopled with faceless strangers. Now I could imagine Tom Fox hovering over a powerful politician as he snipped at the man's hair. For Tom was one of the unlikeliest missionaries to the mighty I would come to know in those years between the flights. Tom is a barber in the Cannon House of Representatives Office Building, and has been for 20 years. For 30 years he has been working with the mighty heads of Washington, cutting their hair, and trying to fill them with Good News.

I had gotten to know Tom through the prayer breakfast movement. He has been head usher for the National Prayer Breakfast for more than 20 years.

Tom Fox started his Washington barbering at age 22. In those days he trimmed hair at the General Officers Club, where one of his customers was a tough Army general, Dwight David Eisenhower.

"As a general, Mr. Eisenhower was quite flamboyant," said Fox. "But after he went into the White House and was baptized at National Presbyterian Church, he really grew in stature."

Fox also cut the hair of the man who was to become Eisenhower's Vice President—Richard Nixon. Fox talked often with Nixon about spiritual things. Nixon once told him he had made a profession of faith at a crusade in Minneapolis under evangelist Paul Rader.

"Nixon, as I look back now, was two people," Fox recalled. "The one I knew was a fine man; the other one I didn't know. There were just two sides to the man."

Then there was Lyndon Johnson. Through the

years of their relationship, he and Fox became fast friends. Fox even became a spiritual advisor of sorts to the President.

During Johnson's presidency, Fox was head usher at the National City Christian Church, not far from the White House. Johnson wanted to get back to church, and Tom recommended that he try National City Christian.

Not only did Johnson try it, but many Sundays Tom Fox would ride to the church with the President. For the eight years of Johnson's stay in the White House, Fox accompanied him to a number of religious activities.

Toward the end of his presidency, Johnson seemed to have made a rededication of himself. "During his last year in the White House, I'd watch him sit in church and cry," said Fox.

According to Fox, Gerald Ford probably had the most stable spiritual background of the five presidents he has known and barbered. "Jerry Ford really loves the Lord, but he doesn't wear his religion on his sleeve. I know he went to the Lord a lot in his two years in the White House. He's really experienced the New Birth, and it's been that way a long time," Tom said.

Fox obviously feels at ease sharing Christ with some of the most powerful people on earth. There is a reason for that. "I've never thought of them as big people," he said. "I started working with them when I was so young, I don't get afraid with them. They're just normal human beings to me. And I'm not ashamed of being a Christian. I just take these guys like I find them. By doing that, I can talk to them.''

I wondered on this swing into Washington: Has Tom Fox' talking done any good? Has the Fellowship Foundation really been used of God to change anything? Will it make any difference that Rolfe McCollister and Bill Bright and Swede Anderson are in Washington? Can the Sojourners really do anything to change the lifestyle of a significant number of people? Will *Dunamis* make any real difference?

In sum, after all the wheels have spun, groups have met, Bible passages been studied, prayers said, is it really worth it?

Yes.

In thinking of the years since I had first come to Washington, and the sometimes big, sometimes small spiritual revolutions I had witnessed, that was the only conclusion I could draw.

I could remember too many things about some of my own colleagues. There had been that day in 1973 when I attended a conference on Christian leadership with a fellow White House staffer I thought was a new Christian. His name was Egil Krogh. I did not know it then, but he would later—in just weeks—be revealed as head of the infamous ''plumbers unit'' of the White House. I listened to Krogh as he testified to a group of business leaders of his new discoveries in Christ. Later, that same faith would buoy him through the rigors of Watergate and a jail sentence.

There was Jeb Magruder. I remembered him as a

bright young comer, carrying out the commands of his boss of the Nixon campaign, John Mitchell. I recalled a late afternoon meeting when Magruder seemed almost a zombie, a man stretched to the limit with burden. The Watergate revelations would show why Magruder was so burdened. But he left prison to work with Young Life, a Christian organization for youth. Magruder had been touched by that network of missionaries to the mighty.

And there was no way I could forget Chuck Colson. This return trip to Washington, in fact, was for a meeting with Colson on his prison ministry. But I remembered the day when a friend had called from Washington and told me about Colson's receiving Christ. I remembered another day when another friend called and told me Colson had been transferred to the Federal Prison Camp just 150 miles from my home to serve the rest of his Watergate-related sentence. My friend asked if I would visit Colson periodically and keep up the sharing ministry they had begun with him. And I remembered Colson's prayers in a tiny conference room at the prison.

And there had been so many others from those dark days which became days of light because people found Christ—people like James McCord and Julie Nixon Eisenhower.

At last there was me. On this day as I flew into Washington, I was pastor of a church, something I would never have been doing had people in Washington not touched me in Christian witness. I had been a low-level aide at the White House who thought things were wrapped up. Then Doug Coe moved in with his ministry, and God began stirring in me with hungerings for Him I had not let myself feel in years.

Someone has said that when sin is its ugliest, Grace is its prettiest. The Cross was the most graphic proof of that. And so was the Watergate period. There has been much criticism of the religious changes that occurred in its wake. But what the critics miss is that these missionaries to the mighty have been laying the groundwork of witness and prayer for so long, that when sin bottomed out, there was a place for people in Washington to go. God reaped the spiritual fruits of the Watergate harvest-time through those heroic folk who had been working quietly for so long!

And He continues to do the same thing.

My main objective in this book has not been to critique what Christians are doing in Washington, though that has sneaked in here and there. Essentially, I have just wanted to show some of the exciting things God is doing. But I do have some concerns about the ministries, if they are to continue with effectiveness.

For one thing, it is imperative that Christian workers in Washington recognize that *God diversifies His Body of believers for different tasks.*

Some Christian observers are perplexed at the Washington scene. Why does the Christian commitment of Senator Mark Hatfield angle him slightly toward the left, while that of Senator John Stennis seems to place him on the conservative side? People often wrongly conclude that one or the other is not really committed to Christ.

There is room for both a liberal and a conservative stance among Christian politicians. If one is in Christ, his deepest values are not derived from any ideological system. They come from Christ. Sometimes that will elicit a conservative response, and sometimes it will produce a liberal stance— depending on the issue.

Consequently, participants in the Washington ministries should find in Christ their point of unity, no matter what their basic political philosophy. If those to whom they minister need changing, how else can that happen except by bringing them into contact with Christ?

The missionaries to the mighty must *skirt the temptation to deal only with broad abstractions of ethics.* At some point they must take their stance and minister squarely in the name of Christ.

The counterpart of cultural religion is a mushy faith that has no ultimate reference point. It cares for congressmen and White House aides and Hill secretaries and assorted bureaucrats, but it never tells them *why* it cares. At some point, the wraps must be removed and Christ must be shared if the ministry is to be authentically Christian.

One Washington group several years ago felt strongly impressed to ask a non-Christian to speak at a prayer meeting. They felt the person would be able to relate to some others who were guests, and they to him. But members of the sponsoring group also used the opportunity of the invitation to sit down with the speaker-to-be and share Christ with him. The result was that his remarks centered on Christ. He had no doubt as to where the sponsoring group was coming from nor why they were interested in him.

Further, Washington Christians must ask the Holy Spirit to help them *recognize cultural religion when they see it, and avoid it at all costs.*

Essentially, cultural religion is that kind of faith which emphasizes the preservation of the human institutions which help maintain a society and which reflects the values of its culture without challenging them. Perhaps the best biblical example of cultural religion is found in Amos 7. There, Amaziah, the court priest to King Jereboam, ordered Amos the prophet out of the sanctuary of God, because Amos was speaking out against the king. And Amaziah even went so far as to tell Amos that Beth-El—literally, "God's house"—was "the king's sanctuary, a royal palace" (Amos 7:13 NEB)!

Cultural religion is closely akin to the Sunday morning faith of many church members. They run through the rituals and motions during the allotted time on Sundays. But there is no application of the worship experience nor its message beyond that.

Such a flimsy faith can sneak up on groups trying to minister in Washington. It can even come from the very earnest desire to cultivate a new individual for ministry. In the process of building the relationship, the missionary to the mighty has to watch that he does not simply affirm every position and statement a politician makes. Sometimes the institutions of ministry—as suggested by Sojourners and *Dunamis*—must take the risk, speak the biblical message, and let the chips fall where they will!

Another pitfall the missionaries to the mighty must sidestep is that of *not limiting their ministries to the mighty.* In God's eyes, a person needs Christ whether he is driven through Washington in a limousine or rides a bicycle up Pennsylvania Avenue.

Obviously, some groups feel their special task is working with officialdom. But that kingdom encompasses a lot of levels! Hardly anyone in Washington yields more power than the bureaucrat charged with implementing the decisions of the mighty.

To me, nothing came closer to stifling the spirit of our White House prayer group than this attitude. One of the staff secretaries found out about our meetings and asked if she could come. I readily agreed, and she became a regular. But one day I received a call from one of my colleagues. The lady should not be invited any more, he suggested. The prayer group should be limited to that class in the White House cosmos known as "professionals." Happily, as we noted earlier, that attitude has changed to some extent.

Finally, it seems important that the *church and para-church groups not see themselves as separate entities working for separate goals.* To put it another way, para-church organizations should not view themselves as having a monopoly on ministry in Washington, nor should the churches. Some of the para-church organizations, for example, try to exclude all but a few clergymen from their activities.

They are afraid the preachers will frighten off the people to whom the groups want to minister. Though there may be some basis for this fear, para-church groups should guard against it.

The spirit that can be developed between church and para-church organizations in Washington is that of servanthood. They should view themselves as servants of one another. The churches can provide spiritual resources to the para-church organizations. They can provide mechanisms of ministry not available to the churches.

Perhaps nothing more is needed than periodic information and discussion meetings between leaders of the para-church groups and pastors. A pastors' organization might take the lead in setting up encounters to inform the various parts of Christ's Body of what the other parts are doing!

Rather than seeing themselves as competitors for the souls of the mighty, the various ministry forms in Washington can evaluate their own aims and methods in the light of what their colleagues are doing. In Washington as nowhere else in America is the delicate but certain tension between different forms of ministry so important.

The nation did not have the advantage of such a diversity of approach early in this century. There was hardly anyone to yank Senator Albert J. Beveridge, and anchor him to sound theology, when, in 1900, he said this: "For God's hand was in [American expansion overseas]. His plans were working out [its] glorious result. And just as futile is resistance to the continuance today of the American people toward the mastery of the world. This is a destiny neither vague nor undesirable. It is definite, splendid and holy."

Beveridge's speech echoed the American messianic consciousness, which can be traced back as far as Puritans like John Winthrop. He skirted across the Atlantic in 1630, his eyes probing the horizon for the soft rising lines of Massachusetts, which he expected to be a New Israel.

As Christianity developed in America, biblical conservatives were espousing the messianic consciousness for the new society. Even Dwight L. Moody, and his predecessor in evangelism, Jonathan Edwards, tended to preach the American messianic consciousness.

The liberals in American Christian thought emphasized the "kingdom." Robert T. Handy, in *Review and Expositor* (Winter, 1976, p. 54) noted that "Though there were many variations in detail, in general the idea of the kingdom that became popular among Protestant liberals in the late nineteenth century was that of a perfected society on earth emerging through a combination of natural and spiritual means." And there was no doubt that the beginnings of that "perfect society" for many nineteenth century liberals would be in the United States.

The messianic consciousness was there in John Kennedy's famous inaugural speech in 1961: "The energy, the faith, the devotion which we bring to this endeavor will light our country and all who serve it, and the glow from that fire can truly light the world."

The language of messianism shifted in the seventies. The terse rythms of technology became the new messianic expression. But the consciousness was still there.

Now there is a tension, a frustration. It revolves around a crumbling sense of identity. For whether it was right or wrong for America to grow up with a messianic consciousness, that is precisely what it did. Yet now it finds itself in an era of atheistic humanism—a bankrupt humanism already depleted yet with that messianism still gnawing at its soul. And the crisis is this: We have a messianism without a messiah!

But there *is* a Messiah, One Who lives not to build great nations, but to build great people. Great nations are often the fruit of His Presence. But the base of the work of the missionaries to the mighty must never be anything else but that expressed by Tom Fox: "They're just normal human beings who need the Lord."